THE AMERICAN KENNEL CLUB'S
Meet the
Bulldog™

The Responsible Dog Owner's Handbook

AKC's Meet the Breeds Series

BOWTIE
P R E S S®
Irvine, California
A Division of BowTie, Inc.

AN OFFICIAL PUBLICATION OF THE AMERICAN KENNEL CLUB

AMERICAN KENNEL CLUB™

Brought to you by The American Kennel Club and The Bulldog Club of America.
Lead Editor: Karen Julian
Art Director: Cindy Kassebaum
Production Supervisor: Jessica Jaensch

Vice President, Chief Content Officer: June Kikuchi
Vice President, Kennel Club Books: Andrew DePrisco
BowTie Press: Jennifer Calvert, Amy Deputato, Karen Julian, Jarelle S. Stein

Photographs by: Blackhawk Productions (Dwight Dyke): Cover inset, 37, 43, 46, 52, 55, 109, 116, 118; BowTie Studio: Back cover, 16, 18, 21, 23, 32, 39, 54, 58, 72, 74, 76, 80, 100, 124; Close Encounters of the Furry Kind (Jeannie Harrison): 3, 4, 6, 9, 14, 24, 31, 44, 51, 64, 120; Diane Lewis Photography: Cover inset, 4, 26, 36, 41, 45, 56, 65, 108; Fox Hill Photo (Paulette Johnson): 34, 40, 60, 66, 70, 71, 75, 77, 82, 86, 87, 90, 92, 93, 96, 97, 98, 99, 103; LMEimages (Laurie Meehan-Elmer): Cover, 4, 13, 29, 42, 48, 50, 67, 84, 88, 89, 94, 95, 104, 112, 114, 117; Mark Raycroft Photogrpahy: Cover insets, 1, 8, 10, 12, 22, 28, 30, 33, 38, 59, 62, 63, 68, 79, 106, 110, 111, 121; Natural Balance Inc.: 119; Noppadol Paothong: 61.

BowTie Press®
Division of BOWTIE INC.
3 Burroughs, Irvine, CA 92618

Library of Congress Cataloging-in-Publication Data

The American Kennel Club's meet the bulldog : the responsible dog owner's handbook.
    p. cm.
 Includes bibliographical references and index.
 ISBN 978-1-935484-87-5
1. Bulldog. I. American Kennel Club. II. Title: Meet the bulldog.
 SF429.B85A44 2012
 636.72--dc23
                          2011053045

Printed and bound in the United States
15 14 13 12   1 2 3 4 5 6 7 8 9 10

Meet Your New Dog

Welcome to *Meet the Bulldog*. Whether you're a long-time Bulldog owner, or you've just brought home your first puppy, we wish you a lifetime of happiness and enjoyment with your new pet.

In this book, you'll learn about the history of the breed, receive tips on feeding, grooming, and training, as well as learn about all the fun you can have with your dog. The American Kennel Club and BowTie Press hope that this book serves as a useful guide on the lifelong journey you'll take with your canine companion.

Owned and cherished by millions across America, Bulldogs make wonderful companions and also enjoy taking part in a variety of dog sports, including Conformation (dog shows), Obedience, Rally®, and Agility.

Thousands of Bulldogs have also earned the AKC Canine Good Citizen® certification by demonstrating their good manners at home and in the community. We hope that you and your Bulldog will become involved in AKC events, too! Learn how to get involved at www .akc.org/events or find a training club in your area at www.akc.org/events/trainingclubs.cfm.

We encourage you to connect with other Bulldog owners on the AKC website (www.akc .org), Facebook (www.facebook.com/american kennelclub), and Twitter (@akcdoglovers). Also visit the website for the Bulldog Club of America (www.thebca.org), the national parent club for the Bulldog, to learn about the breed from reputable exhibitors and breeders.

Enjoy *Meet the Bulldog*!

Sincerely,

Dennis B. Sprung
AKC President and CEO

6

46

56

112

Contents

CHAPTER ONE

For the Love of a Bulldog

Once stereotypically known as a bullbaiting dog, the Bulldog is now favored as a devoted, lovable family companion. In spite of his rough-and-tumble roots, the gentle, wrinkly Bulldog exists for purely one reason—to keep his family happy! The Bulldog is a very special and unique breed, and each dog possesses a charming personality all his own.

As part of the AKC's Non-Sporting Group, the Bulldog keeps company with such breeds as

History in the Making

The Bulldog Club of America (BCA), the breed's parent club, was founded in 1890, about thirty years after sports like dog fighting and bullbaiting were legally banned in England. A group of Bulldog fanciers decided that the breed shouldn't disappear, and the first Bulldog club was born. The BCA's objective was, and still is, to promote the breed and provide education and exhibition opportunities.

the French Bulldog, Boston Terrier, and Poodle—all known for their doting, companion-dog qualities. In recent years, the Bulldog has gained popularity in the United States, rising to tenth on the list of top dog breeds (according to American Kennel Club registrations) in 2007, the first time since 1935, and moving up to sixth in 2011. The Bulldog is well-known and very recognizable with his thickset, sturdy frame and distinguished, sweet demeanor. With a Bulldog next to you, there's no doubt that you will run across someone who will recognize the breed and immediately exclaim with a big smile, "Oh! A Bulldog!"

THE REAL BULLDOG

There are quite a few old wives' tales about the Bulldog, stemming from assumptions about the breed's personality and physical appearance. Most of those stereotypes are completely false! Let's take the time to set the record straight on the Bulldog's real characteristics and needs.

A Lover, Not a Fighter

Though it's true that the breed was once used as a bullbaiting guard dog, the Bulldog's attitude and demeanor are anything but aggressive. Known (and loved) for their calm and passive personalities, Bulldogs are utterly devoted to their families. Weighing in at 40 to 65 pounds, a Bulldog is not a lap dog—but that won't stop him from trying!

Are you looking for a companion that will live in the house with you and will want to spend every waking hour with the family? Are you interested in a dog

Gentle and loving, a Bulldog's main purpose is to be a companion. The breed's sturdy frame and broad chest are very recognizable.

that will always be with you, sit next to you, and follow you around the house? Then the Bulldog is for you! You can't leave this dog alone for hours in the yard and expect him to be content. He is a companion dog, meaning that he expects and needs your companionship and attention.

The Bulldog is not a guard dog! If this is what you are looking for, you should consider another breed. Keep in mind, while he does not make a good guard dog, the Bulldog is watchful and devoted to his people—and his looks alone may deter any would-be intruder!

The Bulldog is excellent with children, and he will quickly become a playful companion to your little ones. But like all other dogs, he first needs to be taught how to treat his new young family members, just as the kids must be taught how to treat him. Encourage your children to interact with your new puppy calmly, quietly, and gently. They cannot ride on his back, startle him, pull his ears, or otherwise handle him roughly. Interactions between the dog and the kids should always be supervised, and with proper training, your Bulldog will grow into the oversized lover that he naturally is.

What a Looker!

The Bulldog is a medium-sized, short-muzzled breed with wide shoulders and a formidable stance. With a massive head, sturdy legs, and wrinkles covering his body, this is a breed that requires little coat care other than a thorough brushing a few times a week, but he will need special attention to keep his skin folds clean,

Did You Know?

The Bulldog's tough appearance naturally makes the breed a symbol of strength, tenacity, and adaptability. The Bulldog has been adopted as the official mascot of several well-known institutions, such as Mack Trucks and the United States Marine Corps.

All dogs need exercise, and the burly Bulldog is no exception. Bulldogs need at least one or two walks a day and lots of playtime to stay fit and healthy.

especially those on his face. Although grooming is minimal for this breed, as a Bulldog owner, you must regularly brush his coat, trim his nails, check his ears and eyes, brush his teeth, and clean his wrinkles. You need to devote time and effort to keep your dog clean, healthy, and smelling good. Are you willing to do this for your Bulldog?

The Bulldog requires extra care because, like the Boston Terrier, Boxer, and several other breeds, he is a brachycephalic breed. These dogs have flat faces, wide heads, and short muzzles. Bulldogs are sensitive to extreme temperatures and must not be allowed too much time outdoors in heat and humidity. You will need to pay careful attention to your Bulldog in both the heat and cold.

As a short-muzzled breed, a Bulldog's respiratory system differs from that of longer-nosed breeds, such as the German Shepherd Dog or Labrador Retriever. Although the Bulldog's unique shape may not win him any races, this is a dog built for stamina, not speed. Bulldogs successfully participate in AKC dog sports like agility and obedience. They enjoy activity just as much as more athletic breeds, but they do not tolerate strenuous workouts. Moderate exercise will keep your Bulldog physically and mentally healthy and happy. And never forget, his amiable personality makes him a great candidate for therapy work.

With a Brain to Match

The Bulldog is dearly loved for his disposition, good looks, intelligence, and devotion to his family. Bulldogs are inquisitive, active, affable dogs. It's no wonder that Winston Churchill was called the "British Bulldog." Like the venerable statesman, the Bulldog is extremely smart. And he prefers his owner to be at least as sharp as he is. That being said, all dogs need lessons in manners. Basic obedience training will not only transform your dog into a good canine citizen but will also stimulate your smart pup both physically and mentally. Good training takes time and dedication, and you must work with your Bulldog on a daily basis to have an obedient dog with good manners.

THE RIGHT CHOICE

Before purchasing a Bulldog, think about the personality and characteristics of the breed to determine if this is the dog that you want to join your family. Ask yourself: Do you have the time needed to give to a dog? Will you help him grow and thrive both physically and mentally? Are you willing to train your dog and teach him good manners? Answer these questions honestly before deciding if a Bulldog is the right breed for you.

Your Bulldog should have at least two outings a day, such as a walk or a light jog in the morning and again in the evening. He will need moderate exercise,

Bulldog Temperament

Despite their fierce history, Bulldogs are actually very gentle, mellow dogs that get along well with children and most other pets. They are extremely loving of their human families, shadowing the footsteps of their owners wherever they go. Sometimes stubborn, but extremely intelligent and always willing to please, a Bulldog is very good-natured and trainable. The Bulldog is a wrinkly gentleman, and he is the perfect addition to a household in need of a devoted, playful canine friend and companion.

Get to Know the AKC

The country's leading canine organization, the American Kennel Club is a nonprofit organization dedicated to the betterment and promotion of purebred dogs as family companions. The AKC is the largest and most prestigious dog registry in the United States. It was founded in 1884 with the mission of "upholding its registry and promoting the sport of purebred dogs and breeding for type and function." Supporting everything from health and wellness to breeding standards to fun activities for the whole family, the AKC thrives on the participation of dog lovers like you.

Help continue the legacy by registering your purebred Bulldog with the AKC. It's as simple as filling out the Dog Registration Application you received when you bought your puppy and mailing it to the AKC in North Carolina, or register online at www.akc.org/reg.

Bulldog Therapy

Therapy dogs typically visit hospitals, nursing homes, and assisted living facilities where the dog's social instincts combine with the healing effects of canine companionship. It's been scientifically proven that petting a dog can reduce stress and lower blood pressure. The therapeutic effects of this irresistible tub of love come as no surprise to fanciers of the Bulldog breed. When we're feeling under the weather, a slobbery kiss or snuggle from a sensitive Bulldog can be the best medicine. As a bonus, a Bulldog in the role of therapy dog does a lot to dispel any misconceptions that the breed is aloof or unfriendly. As with most misconceptions, the idea that a Bulldog is unsociable is no doubt perpetrated by those who have not met one.

In recent years, the Bulldog has gained popularity in the United States and is now the sixth most popular breed in the country.

What Is a Parent Club?

AMERICAN KENNEL CLUB™

Breed standards are written by experienced breeders across the country who belong to that particular breed's parent club. A parent club is a national organization recognized by the American Kennel Club that represents a particular dog breed. The Bulldog standard was written by the Bulldog Club of America, which is the AKC parent club of the Bulldog breed. You can learn more about the Bulldog Club of America at its website, www.thebca.org.

training, and grooming. The fast-growing Bulldog must be fed on a consistent schedule and requires optimal nutrition to develop properly. Adding a puppy to your life is a big decision, and one that should be considered carefully and only made after thorough research.

For more information on the Bulldog, check out other books on the breed and talk to breeders and owners. Bulldog people are happy to give advice about their beloved breed. Although the internet can be a wonderful tool, it contains a lot of bad information, too. The best resources on the breed are the American Kennel Club (www.akc.org) and the breed's national parent club, the Bulldog Club of America (www.thebca.org). These organizations' websites will direct you to local Bulldog clubs in your region.

Is a Bulldog right for you? Find out about the breed and talk to Bulldog owners before committing to bringing home this sweetheart of a dog.

At a Glance ...

A Non-Sporting dog by AKC classification, the Bulldog's sole job is to be a devoted and faithful companion. Don't let his shape and size fool you, the Bulldog is a fun-loving breed that can take part in a variety of sports and activities.

· ·

The Bulldog is a gentle and playful breed that will follow on the heels of his owner. Bulldogs are intelligent and kind dogs that are well suited for families with children and for community service such as canine assistance and therapy work.

· ·

Brachycephalic breeds like the Bulldog have short muzzles, which require extra supervision due to their sensitivity to extreme temperatures and humidity.

· ·

Be honest in assessing your lifestyle and your compatibility with the Bulldog breed, as well as your level of commitment to dog ownership as a whole. Get all the information and advice you can on the Bulldog so you can make an educated decision.

CHAPTER TWO

The Undeniable Bulldog

he Bulldog is a beautiful and recognizable breed, enduring as a popular choice with fanciers, breeders, and pet owners who embrace it's unique brand of appeal with good reason. The Bulldog is loyal, loving, gentle, and intelligent—everything you could want in a companion, wrapped up in one sturdy, wrinkly package. To know the Bulldog is to love him. But to really understand this popular breed, you have to know its history.

Colleges love the Bulldog—more than forty claim the breed as their mascot. The most well-known are Yale's Handsome Dan, Georgetown's Jack the Bulldog, and the University of Georgia's Uga.

The Bulldog is a nearly ancient breed that descends from a long line of tough dogs originally used for bullbaiting and bearbaiting. He may have started with a tougher-than-nails background, but the Bulldog is now considered the national dog of England and a beloved family pet around the world.

BULLDOG ORIGINS

In order to understand the Bulldog and his background, you must first learn a bit about the history of the fighting dog. Bullbaiting began in England as early as the mid-1300s. The cruel "sport" of baiting pitted animal against animal—bears, lions, monkeys, bulls, and eventually dog against dog—and was very popular among the wealthy as well as commoners, who had little in the way of entertainment. The average peasant could breed a tough dog, send it into the ring with a bull, and take bets on which animal would win. People of all classes found these

A PIECE OF HISTORY

The Bulldog became the official mascot of the Marine Corps in 1922. In 1957, the Bulldog mascot first acquired the name "Chesty," after the highly-decorated Lieutenant General Lewis "Chesty" Puller. Since then, there have been twelve Bulldogs—all named Chesty—who have served in the Marine Corps, including one female! The current USMC mascot is Chesty XIII.

gambling matches entertaining, and it allowed peasants to make a bit of money in the process.

Dogs at that time were not bred for their looks but rather for toughness, tenacity, and spirit. The Bulldog that could pin a bull in the least amount of time, regardless of any injury to himself, became a prize, particularly if he could repeat this feat time after time. This dog was then bred to an equally tough dog with the hope of raising dogs that were as ferocious as the parents, or even more so, in the bullbaiting ring.

By the early 1800s, a group of individuals fought to stop the cruel and inhumane fighting of animals for sport, and laws were passed that eventually outlawed the practice. In 1835, all dog fighting was outlawed in England. The Bulldog experienced a decline in popularity as a result, as owners no longer felt that these dogs had a purpose.

By 1860, dog shows were being held in England and a small group of fanciers believed that the grand Bulldog of the past should not fall into further decline. This group set about to preserve the Bulldog's desirable characteristics as well as breed out (eliminate) the dog's fighting instincts and other disagreeable traits. In 1875, a breed standard was written by these exhibitors in the United Kingdom, stating just what the Bulldog should look and act like. This gave the breed the start it needed on its road to preservation and, eventually, to popularity.

In addition to this renewed popularity in its homeland, the Bulldog was also becoming a beloved breed in America. By the early 1900s, several wealthy fanciers imported top English champions to their kennels for breeding. Today, the Bulldog remains a very popular dog in the United States as well as in England

What's in a Name

Originally bred in the British Isles, today's Bulldogs were commonly known as English Bulldogs until the 1920s. As the Bulldog breed became more popular in the United States, the American Kennel Club eventually dropped the "English" from the breed's official name.

Meet the Bulldog

AKC Meet the Breeds®, hosted by the American Kennel Club and presented by PetPartners, Inc., is a great place to see Bulldogs, as well as more than 200 other dog and cat breeds. Not only can you see dogs, cats, puppies, and kittens of all sizes, you can also talk to experts in each of the breeds. Meet the Breeds™ features demonstration rings to watch events for law enforcement K9s, grooming, agility, and obedience. You also can browse the more than 100 vendor booths for every imaginable pet product for you and your Bulldog.

It's great fun for the whole family. AKC Meet the Breeds takes place in the fall in New York City. Meet the Breeds also sponsors a smaller event at the AKC Eukanuba National Championship each winter in Orlando. For more information, check out www.meetthebreeds.com.

STOP

WITHERS

BACK

MUZZLE

CHEST

ELBOW

BRISKET

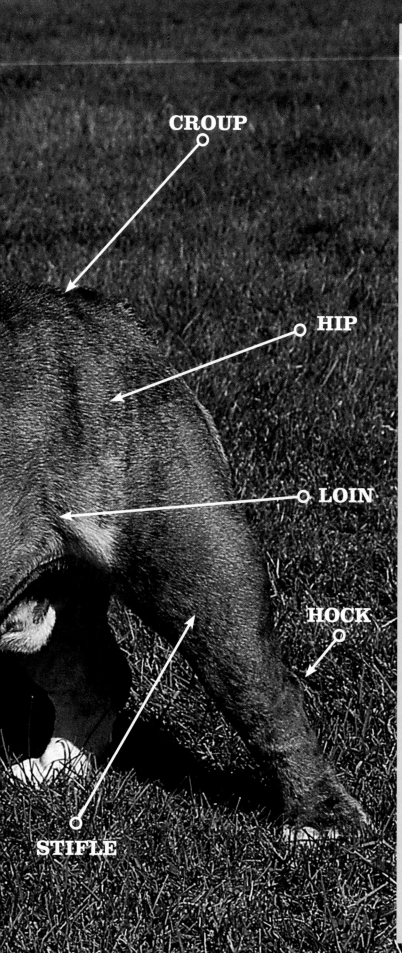

CROUP

HIP

LOIN

HOCK

STIFLE

The Bulldog in Brief

COUNTRY OF ORIGIN:
England

ORIGINAL PURPOSE:
Bullbaiting and bearbaiting

GROUP:
Non-Sporting

AVERAGE LIFE SPAN:
8 to 10 years

COAT:
Short, flat, glossy, and smooth; loose all over the body with heavy facial wrinkles.

COLOR:
All shades of brindle (red most desirable in the show ring), solid white, solid red, fawn or fallow, and piebald (large patches of two or more colors). Solid black is not desirable.

GROOMING:
Bulldogs must be brushed weekly, and the wrinkles on their faces and bodies must be cleaned daily.

HEIGHT/WEIGHT:
Approximately 14 to 15 inches at the withers; between 40 and 65 pounds.

TRAINABILITY:
Moderate

PERSONALITY:
Easygoing, affectionate, and intelligent; sometimes stubborn, but always loyal and willing to please.

ACTIVITY LEVEL:
Low to moderate. Bulldogs are sensitive to extreme temperatures.

GOOD WITH OTHER PETS:
Yes, with proper introductions.

NATIONAL BREED CLUB:
Bulldog Club of America; www .thebca.org

RESCUE:
Bulldog Club of America Rescue Network; www.rescuebulldogs.org

The lure of adorable Bulldog puppies is powerful, but remember that there are adult dogs in need of loving homes, too. If you want to skip the potty training and chewing mishaps, an adult Bulldog may be the best option for you.

Adult dogs often need new homes for a variety of reasons. Elderly owners die, leaving their pets unowned. Breeders may have adult dogs that can no longer be bred or dogs that are unsuitable for breeding. Retired show dogs also may be available for adoption.

So where do you begin a search for an adult Bulldog? While the internet has numerous pet adoption sites, most do not have purebred Bulldogs. If you want to adopt a Bulldog, start with the parent club, the Bulldog Club of America (www.thebca.org), and search for Bulldog-specific rescues.

and elsewhere around the world. Within the American Kennel Club, the Bulldog has steadily moved up the ranks in popularity and broke into the top ten breeds in 2007, according to AKC registration numbers.

A DISTINGUISHED GENTLEMAN

What makes a Bulldog look like a Bulldog? And how did the Bulldog come to look and act as he does today? Every breed of dog registered with the AKC has an official breed standard, which is a written description that details how an ideal representative of the breed should look and act. All breed standards are written by a committee of members selected by the national breed club. For the Bulldog, the breed standard was written and shaped by the Bulldog Club of America (www.thebca.org), the national breed club sanctioned by the AKC.

In personality, the Bulldog is a lively, intelligent, and confident dog that is very affectionate, devoted, loyal, and, of course, very loving. The breed standard itself describes the Bulldog as "kind" and "courageous," an ideal companion breed well-placed within the Non-Sporting Group. The Non-Sporting Group includes a range of very diverse breeds of all different shapes and sizes, such as the Chow Chow, Dalmatian, Bichon Frise, and Shiba Inu. A characteristic that all Non-Sporting breeds share, however, is loyalty and devotion to their owners and a companionable personality.

A LOVABLE MUG

A Bulldog's head and face is one of the most recognizable of all breeds. Like the rest of his body, the Bulldog's head is very large and square, with small ears and dark eyes. A Bulldog's eyes should be round and of moderate size, neither bulging nor sunken in. The ears are set high on the head. The most desirable ear for the Bulldog is the rose ear, which is a small drop ear that folds over and back so that the burr of the ear (the inside of the ear) is revealed. The Bulldog should have a large black nose; a brown or liver-colored nose is a disqualification from the show ring. Of course, he will have a massive, broad, square jaw with large, strong teeth meeting in an undershot (lower jaw protrudes beyond the upper) bite, revealing the familiar mug we all know so well.

The Bulldog is a brachycephalic breed, with an extremely short muzzle. This is an important trait of the breed, and also an important aspect to remember as a pet owner. Brachycephalic breeds are very sensitive to extreme temperatures. Bulldog owners must keep a close watch over their dogs to be sure they don't become overheated or overexerted. A Bulldog's body is meant for stamina, not speed. As they say, "Slow and steady wins the race"—and most Bulldogs prefer not to race at all!

UNIQUELY BULLDOG

The Bulldog has a dignified demeanor and should look very sturdy. This medium-sized breed weighs about 50 pounds as an adult male and 40 pounds as an adult female. The Bulldog has a short, very thick, deep, strong neck, and his body holds a well-rounded rib cage. His topline (line of the back from the withers, or shoulders, to the rump) differs from that of many breeds, as he has a

Responsible Pet Ownership

AMERICAN KENNEL CLUB™

Getting a dog is exciting, but it's also a huge responsibility. That's why it's important to educate yourself on all that is involved in being a good pet owner. As a part of the Canine Good Citizen® test, the AKC has a "Responsible Dog Owner's Pledge," which states:

I will be responsible for my dog's health needs.

- ☐ I will provide routine veterinary care, including check-ups and vaccines.
- ☐ I will offer adequate nutrition through proper diet and clean water at all times.
- ☐ I will give daily exercise and regularly bathe and groom.

I will be responsible for my dog's safety.

- ☐ I will properly control my dog by providing fencing where appropriate, by not letting my dog run loose, and by using a leash in public.
- ☐ I will ensure that my dog has some form of identification when appropriate (which may include collar tags, tattoos, or microchip identification).
- ☐ I will provide adequate supervision when my dog and children are together.

I will not allow my dog to infringe on the rights of others.

- ☐ I will not allow my dog to run loose in the neighborhood.
- ☐ I will not allow my dog to be a nuisance to others by barking while in the yard, in a hotel room, etc.
- ☐ I will pick up and properly dispose of my dog's waste in all public areas, such as on the grounds of hotels, on sidewalks, in parks, etc.
- ☐ I will pick up and properly dispose of my dog's waste in wilderness areas, on hiking trails, on campgrounds, and in off-leash parks.

I will be responsible for my dog's quality of life.

- ☐ I understand that basic training is beneficial to all dogs.
- ☐ I will give my dog attention and playtime.
- ☐ I understand that owning a dog is a commitment in time and caring.

The Bulldog Breed Standard

AMERICAN
KENNEL CLUB™

GENERAL APPEARANCE: The perfect Bulldog must be of medium size with a smooth coat; heavy, thick-set, low-swung body; massive short-faced head; wide shoulders; and sturdy limbs. The general appearance and attitude should suggest great stability, vigor, and strength.

HEAD

The eyes, seen from the front, should be situated low down in the skull, as far from the ears as possible. . . . They should be quite round in form, of moderate size, neither sunken nor bulging, and in color should be very dark. . . . The ears should be set high in the head, the front inner edge of each ear joining the outline of the skull at the top back corner of skull, so as to place them as wide apart, and as high, and as far from the eyes as possible. In size they should be small and thin.

The shape termed "rose ear" is the most desirable. . . .The skull should be very large, and in circumference, in front of the ears, should measure at least the height of the dog at the shoulders. . . . The cheeks should be well rounded, protruding sideways and outward beyond the eyes. . . . The face, measured from the front of the cheekbone to the tip of the nose, should be extremely short, the muzzle being very short, broad, turned upward and very deep from the corner of the eye to the corner of the mouth. . . . The nose should be large, broad and black, its tip set back deeply between the eyes. . . . The jaws should be massive, very broad, square and "undershot," the lower jaw projecting considerably in front of the upper jaw and turning up.

BODY

The brisket and body should be very capacious, with full sides, well-rounded ribs and very deep from the shoulders down to its lowest part, where it joins the chest. It should be well let down between the shoulders and forelegs, giving the dog a broad, low, short-legged appearance. . . . The chest should be very broad, deep and full. The back should be short and strong, very broad at the shoulders and comparatively narrow at the loins. . . . The tail may be either straight or "screwed" (but never curved or curly), and in any case must be short, hung low, with decided downward carriage, thick root and fine tip.

COAT AND SKIN

The coat should be straight, short, flat, close, of fine texture, smooth and glossy. (No fringe, feather or curl.) The skin should be soft and loose, especially at the head, neck and shoulders. The head and face should be covered with heavy wrinkles, and at the throat, from jaw to chest, there should be two loose pendulous folds, forming the dewlap.

COLOR OF COAT

The color of coat should be uniform, pure of its kind and brilliant. The various colors found in the breed are to be preferred in the following order: (1) red brindle, (2) all other brindles, (3) solid white, (4) solid red, fawn or fallow, (5) piebald, (6) inferior qualities of all the foregoing. . . . Solid black is very undesirable, but not so objectionable if occurring to a moderate degree in piebald patches. The brindles to be perfect should have a fine, even and equal distribution of the composite colors.

TEMPERAMENT

The disposition should be equable and kind, resolute and courageous (not vicious or aggressive), and the demeanor should be pacific and dignified. These attributes should be countenanced by the expression and behavior.

—Excerpts from the Bulldog Breed Standard

slightly arched back called a wheel back. His chest should be broad and deep, which will give the dog a short-legged appearance. He may have a straight or screw tail, but the tail should never be curved or curly. His legs are strong and muscular, with moderately sized feet. He has high knuckles, and his toenails should be kept characteristically short and stubby.

The Bulldog's short, flat coat should be smooth and glossy. His skin is loose all over with heavy wrinkling on the head and face. Bulldogs come in a variety of colors and patterns: red brindle (a fine, even distribution of darker color over the red), all other brindles, solid white, solid red, fawn or fallow, and piebald (mostly white with patches of color). Solid black is not desirable in the show ring, but plenty of black Bulldogs make great pets.

CHOOSE WISELY

Before deciding on a Bulldog, ask yourself why you want a dog and imagine yourself and your dream dog interacting in various activities. What do you see yourself doing with your dog? Are you jogging down a beach or playing Frisbee with your pup? Are you lazing around the house with a warm, sleepy dog on your lap? Are you visiting friends and running errands with your lovable canine at your side? These imaginary scenarios will help you determine if a Bulldog is the right fit for your lifestyle.

If you don't mind a snoring, wrinkly companion, the Bulldog is the perfect dog for you!

Because of a Bulldog's stature and structure, he will never be an athlete like a retriever or spaniel, so if you are looking for a workout buddy, the Bulldog is not the right breed for you. But that doesn't mean a Bulldog can't be an active member of your family or within the community. Bulldogs are often mistakenly seen as lazy, unable to keep up with a fast-paced lifestyle. This is completely untrue! Bulldogs enjoy walks with their owners and playful activities with kids. Their calm temperament and patient attitude make them ideal for therapy work and obedience. Yes, it is true that as a Bulldog owner you will need to take special care not to overexert your pup, but with supervision, you can become involved in a variety of activities with your Bulldog, both active and relaxing!

At a Glance ...

The Bulldog descends from baiting dogs of centuries past in England, however, in the 1860s, breeders sought to successfully breed out aggressive behavior in the dog, leaving us with the sweet, even-tempered Bulldog we know and love today.

. . . .

Thanks to dedicated breeders, the Bulldog is stabilized and well-established as a favorite in many countries around the world. The breed currently ranks sixth in popularity in the United States.

. . . .

The Bulldog's breed standard was written and approved by the Bulldog Club of America, the national breed club and official parent club of the Bulldog breed.

CHAPTER THREE

So You Want a Bulldog

You've done your homework, evaluated your lifestyle, researched the breed, and decided that you simply cannot live without a Bulldog. How do you go about finding the right puppy? When looking for a Bulldog, seek out a healthy puppy from a good breeder, who gives considerable thought before breeding his or her dogs. A responsible breeder conducts health screenings, has room in his or her home or kennel for a litter, and has the time

One Size Fits All

With so many variations on a theme, it's easy to get confused and believe you have a certain type of dog when you really have another. Size also complicates matters, with some breeders claiming to have "miniature" Bulldog puppies for sale with inflated price tags to prove it. Do not be taken in by these false claims. A Bulldog is a Bulldog is a Bulldog. There is no official "miniature" Bulldog. These "designer dogs" are usually the result of Bulldogs crossbred with French Bulldogs or Boston Terriers. Attempts to miniaturize a breed often result in health and temperament problems.

and dedication to give to the puppies. Because the Bulldog is a popular breed, there are some unethical breeders who are solely profit motivated and sell poorly bred pups that suffer from atypical temperament and poor health. You must be able to recognize a breeder who is not dedicated to the Bulldog breed.

A breeder/puppy search can be an emotionally trying experience, taxing your patience and willpower. All Bulldog puppies are adorable, and it's easy to fall in love with the first one you see. However, a poor-quality Bulldog will have health and temperament problems that can empty your wallet and break your heart. A reputable, responsible breeder is the only source for a Bulldog puppy. Not only do good breeders dedicate their programs to bettering the breed, but they will also be a resource for you throughout your dog's life. Arm yourself with a list of questions for the breeder and be prepared to answer questions as well.

FINDING THE RIGHT BREEDER

To begin your search, check out the websites for the Bulldog Club of America (www.thebca.org) and the AKC (www.akc.org), and look for breeders and affiliated clubs in your region. You will likely be able to find one in your state. Your local club should be able to provide the name of a responsible breeder or two, as reputable breeders should belong to the AKC Breeder of Merit Program and the Bulldog parent club, as well as regional and local breed clubs. These clubs are very helpful because the members will be able to answer all your questions. A good breeder will be someone who has been breeding for some years and who has had success in conformation (dog shows) and other dog activities.

Networking is another important tool you can use to find a reputable breeder. Tell your friends and relatives that you are looking to add a Bulldog to your family; also check with a local veterinarian for a breeder referral. Use the internet to educate yourself about Bulldogs, but beware, many online sources are not to be trusted. Make sure to follow up your research with the AKC, the BCA, or your local Bulldog club.

BREEDER QUESTIONS

Choosing a breeder is a big decision, just as important as choosing the right puppy. Responsible breeders are dedicated to breeding only the best dogs to preserve the breed according to the breed standard. Good breeders are involved in conformation, obedience, and other AKC sports, and they have awards accredited to their name and kennel. Ask what activities the breeder is currently involved in and to see any awards he or she has achieved. Good breeders should be more than willing to show you how involved they are in the dog sport.

Other questions to ask involve the breeder's history and breeding habits:

• How long have you been breeding Bulldogs? The longer the breeder has been involved in breeding Bulldogs, the better.

• What genetic diseases and health problems most commonly affect the Bulldog? Health issues that are sometimes found in Bulldogs include elongated soft palates, entropian and ectropian (eyelid abnormalities), hip and knee joint issues, and skin allergies. Ask the breeder about these problems and how often they occur in the breed overall and in the breeder's lines specifically. A responsible breeder will know the history of his or her line, and be open to this discussion, rather than saying, "None of my dogs has those problems," or "*My dogs are all healthy.*" Ask the breeder what health testing the sire (father) and dam (mother) have had and if those results are registered with the Orthopedic Foundation for Animals (OFA), a national canine genetic-disease registry, including testing for knees, hips, eyes, and heart. This testing is also an indicator of whether a specific dog is CHIC-certified. CHIC, the Canine Health Information Center, is a centralized canine health database jointly sponsored by the AKC Canine Health Foundation and the OFA. Testing required for CHIC certification varies by breed. Bulldog CHIC testing currently includes patellar luxation evaluation (knees) and cardiac testing.

• Have your puppies been raised in your home? It is important to know where the puppies have been raised because socialization should begin at a very young age. Your breeder should know the temperaments of each of the puppies and have begun introducing them to different people, sounds, and experiences.

• Will you put all of your warranties and guarantees in writing? The breeder should have a purchase contract that formalizes all of his or her promises.

• If it doesn't work out for any reason, will you take the puppy back? The answer to this question should be yes. Responsible breeders put a lot of time and effort into their litters, and every one of their puppies should be special to them.

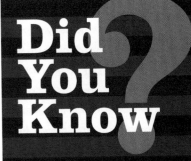

Did You Know?

The Bulldog has been the official company mascot of Mack Trucks, Inc. since World War I, when the British government procured Mack AC model trucks to convey troops to the front lines and supply them with food and equipment. The pugnacious image of a Bulldog graces the grille of every Mack truck on the road today.

Rescue Me

Breed-specific dog rescue has become a widespread operation both as a means of saving dogs' lives and providing needy families with pets. Not all rescued dogs are cases of abuse or neglect, so don't shy away from adopting a rescued Bulldog because you fear he will have behavioral problems. While it is true that some dogs may be rescued from unacceptable living conditions, a stable, loving home is all they need to become happy, wonderful pets. There is no greater gift to a homeless pet than offering him a second chance at affection and security. Learn more about Bulldog rescue at the BCA's Rescue Network, www .rescuebulldogs.org.

QUESTIONS FOR YOU

The breeder will most likely have an application for you to fill out and many questions for you to answer, such as:

- Have you had a dog before? How many have you had, and have you ever owned a Bulldog? Did your dogs live long lives?
- How many children do you have, and what are their ages? Will you take the time to teach your children how to treat the new canine family member?
- If only two full-time employed adults comprise your household, who will be around to tend to the physical and emotional needs of the social Bulldog?
- Do you have a fenced yard?
- Do you want a dog that will live primarily outdoors? The Bulldog's unique breathing structure is not tolerant of temperature extremes, nor is his smooth, short coat sufficient protection against the cold.
- Have you ever done any dog training, and are you willing to go to obedience classes with your dog?
- Are there any other pets in your household?

Do not be offended by the breeder's questions, as he or she has the puppy's best interests in mind. Plus, the breeder has put a lot of time, effort, and resources into the litter, and his or her first priority is to place each puppy in a dog-smart, appropriate household where the Bulldog will be wanted, loved, and cared for.

WHAT TO LOOK FOR

Once you've found a Bulldog breeder or two, contact them and schedule a time to visit the kennels. This is an important step in the acquisition process that should not be skipped, even if the breeder isn't local. The condition of the Bulldogs, the premises, and even the breeders themselves will tell you a lot about the quality of dogs they're breeding. Fortunately, Bulldogs are popular enough that chances are you won't have to travel very far to visit a good breeder.

When you visit the kennel for the first time, be sure to look around. Does the breeder raise the puppies in his or her home or in a separate kennel? Is the area clean and well kept? Is the environment calm and soothing or loud and chaotic? All of these things will have an effect on the health and personality of the puppies.

Often, breeders raise new litters in their home to begin socializing the pups to normal household sounds such as the vacuum cleaner, dishwasher, and television. They also interact with the puppies on a daily basis to get them used to being handled and to begin familiarizing them with humans, both strangers and family alike. Also, keep an eye out for ribbons and awards lining the walls of the breeder's home—a good breeder will be active in the national and local breed clubs as well as local conformation competition.

When you meet the puppies, look beyond their adorable faces. Healthy puppies should be lively and brave, willing to walk toward you with wagging tails. The folds of their skin and their fur should be clean and smell fresh. Their eyes should be bright and alert, not swollen or crusty in any way. Take an extra close look at the puppies' noses and ears. There should be no discharge or leaking. The pups should be well rounded and well fed, but be on the lookout for distended bellies, which may indicate intestinal worms or parasites.

It may be tempting to pick an ill or cowering puppy in the hopes that you can provide him with a better home; but keep in mind that you are choosing a dog for a lifetime. His personality is already beginning to form, and you want to choose a pup that will fit with your family and lifestyle. The best way to do this is to select the healthiest Bulldog you can find.

MEET THE PARENTS

Ask to meet the puppies' parents. Ideally, the kennel will have both the sire and dam on site, though often only the mother of the current litter is in residence. Is her temperament playful and happy, without any fear or shyness? Does she appear healthy and clean? Ask the breeder about both parents' history: Have they been tested for genetic health problems? Reputable breeders should guarantee the health of their puppies with documentation from their veterinarian. Beware of breeders who seem secretive or only bring out puppies one at a time.

Ask to see the AKC registration papers and certified pedigrees of both the sire and dam. If you hope to show your pup or enter licensed competitions, registration with the AKC is necessary. The pedigree should include three to five generations of ancestry. Inquire about any titles in the pedigree. Titles indicate a dog's accomplishments in some area of canine competition, which prove the merits of the dog's ancestors and add to the breeder's credibility. You should see "Ch." in a show puppy's pedigree, indicating that relatives were champions.

CHOOSING A PUPPY

So you've found a kennel that's clean and comfortable for the dogs, a breeder who is forthcoming and responsible, and you've

fallen in love with every Bulldog in the litter. How do you go about making your selection?

The first question to ask yourself is whether you want a show dog or a pet. Some breeders charge more for show dogs and less for pets, but that doesn't mean that a pet-quality puppy is undesirable in any way. It just means that he may not meet the breed standard for conformation purposes. A pet-quality Bulldog can grow up to become a titled obedience dog or simply the greatest family pet ever.

Gender is purely a matter of preference. Besides a slight difference in size—males are about

Get Your Registration and Pedigree

A responsible breeder will be able to provide your family with an American Kennel Club registration form and pedigree.

AKC REGISTRATION: When you buy a Bulldog puppy from a breeder, ask the breeder for an American Kennel Club Dog Registration Application form. The breeder will fill out most of the application for you. When you fill out your portion of the document and mail it to the AKC, you will receive a Registration Certificate proving that your dog is officially part of the AKC. Besides recording your name and your dog's name in the AKC database, registration helps fund the AKC's good works such as canine health research, search-and-rescue teams, educating the public about responsible dog care, and much more.

CERTIFIED PEDIGREE: A pedigree is an AKC certificate proving that your dog is a purebred Bulldog. It shows your puppy's family tree, listing the names of his parents and grandparents. If your dog is registered with the AKC, the organization will have a copy of your dog's pedigree on file, which you can order from its website (www.akc.org). Look for any titles that your Bulldog's ancestors have won, including Champion (conformation), Companion Dog (obedience), Tracking Dog (tracking), and so forth. A pedigree doesn't guarantee the health or personality of a dog, but it's a starting point for picking out a good Bulldog puppy.

10 pounds heavier—both sexes have the same limitless capacity for love. There is no scientific evidence to support the theory that females are more affectionate or that males are more protective of their humans.

Your breeder will also play a big part in helping you choose a puppy. After raising the litter for eight weeks, the breeder knows each of the puppies and their personalities. The breeder can help match the right puppy for your lifestyle. Tell your breeder what you are looking for in a puppy and he or she will help you pick out the best Bulldog puppy for you and your family.

By six to eight weeks old, puppies will already be displaying their own personalities. Choose a puppy that is active and playful. A lethargic puppy may have temperament issues that can manifest later on. Puppies should be comfortable around humans and used to being handled. Pick up each puppy one at a time and give him a once-over. His eyes and nose should be clear of any mucus; his coat should be shiny and clean; and his skin free of sores. The breeder should have an up-to-date record of each puppy's worming and vaccination schedule for you to take home with you.

Often, the right puppy will select you. When a Bulldog pup crawls into your lap, props his tiny paws on your chest, and licks your nose, what else is there to think about?

The breeder knows the pups the best, so trust his or her judgment in matching you with the perfect Bulldog puppy.

WHAT TO EXPECT

After picking out a puppy, your breeder will arrange the best time for you to return to pick up the puppy—usually when the puppy is eight to twelve weeks old. The breeder also will give you an assortment of paperwork to take home with you to read and sign. These documents can be confusing if you do not know what to look for. Here are a few items that are a must from any breeder. If they are not included in your packet, be sure to ask for them before taking your new Bulldog puppy home.

Contract

Most reputable breeders have a puppy sales contract that includes specific health guarantees and reasonable health-related return policies. It should also include the puppy's price and spay/neuter requirements. Your breeder should also agree to accept a puppy back if things do not work out. He or she should be willing to check up on the puppy's progress after the Bulldog goes home with you and should be available if you have questions or problems.

Health Records

Your breeder should provide you with a complete history of your puppy's date of birth and medical records, including any vaccinations and immunizations your puppy has received and any health or genetic testing that your pup has undergone. Take these records with you to your first visit to the veterinarian so they can be included in your pup's permanent health file. Your vet will base your puppy's next vaccinations and treatments off of these records.

Pedigree and Registration Papers

Your puppy's breeder should have already registered the litter with the AKC by the time you take your Bulldog home. When you purchase your puppy, the breeder should provide you with an AKC Dog Registration Application for your puppy. A detailed chart of your dog's parentage, going back several generations, should also be included in the documentation the breeder provides. Make sure you have copies of certificates of health for the parents. You should also receive a bill of sale, which includes the puppy's breed, birth date, sex, registered names of the parents, litter number, breeder's name, date of sale, and the seller's signature. Once you get home, fill out the registration application your breeder provided for your puppy, and mail it to the American Kennel Club. Within a few weeks, you will receive a Registration Certificate.

Why Should You Register with the American Kennel Club?

AMERICAN KENNEL CLUB™

Registering your puppy with the American Kennel Club does more than just certify the lineage of your Bulldog. It helps the AKC do many good things for dogs everywhere, such as promote responsible breeding and support the care and health of dogs throughout the world. As a result of your registration, the AKC is able to inspect kennels across the country, educate dog owners about the importance of training through the Canine Good Citizen® Program, support search-and-rescue canines via the AKC Companion Animal Recovery Canine Support and Relief Fund, teach the public about the importance of responsible dog ownership through publications and the annual AKC Responsible Dog Ownership Days, and much more. Not only is the AKC a respected organization dedicated to the registration of purebred dogs, but it is also devoted to the well-being of dogs everywhere. For more information, go to www.akc.org/reg.

General Care Kit

Caring breeders often send you home with a basic puppy starter kit, which usually includes a sample of the puppy's current food, as well as a booklet or handouts about basic Bulldog puppy care. Some breeders will include a blanket with the scent of the puppy's mother and littermates on it so that you can place this next to him while he sleeps to comfort him in his new home. If you decide to change your puppy's food from what the breeder was feeding him, do so gradually by mixing small amounts of his previous food with the new food over a period of a few weeks. This will help your puppy's sensitive digestive system get used to the change.

Bulldogs may look tough, but they are gentle, sweet-tempered, and entirely devoted to their families.

TAKE THE TIME

Finding a good breeder and the perfect Bulldog puppy will take time. Don't rush into buying a puppy—do your research and learn more about the breed and the breeders in your area. The Bulldog is a popular breed, and as such, there are hundreds of breeders to choose from, not all of them good ones. Keep in mind that even after you find a breeder, there may be a waiting list for a puppy. Don't be discouraged! Be patient and you will soon own the perfect Bulldog puppy.

At a Glance ...

Know what to look for in a reputable breeder and how to recognize signs that a person is less than ethical in his or her breeding practices. Consult reliable sources like the Bulldog Club of America and the AKC in your breeder search.

. . . .

Ask your breeder questions about his or her breeding experience, AKC Breeder of Merit participation, and involvement in AKC activities and conformation. The breeder will likewise have many questions for you to be sure that you will make a worthy owner.

. . . .

When visiting the litter, see where the dogs are kept, and meet the mother, father, and other dogs on the premises. Ask to see the litter's and parents' health certifications and discuss terms of the sale. Be sure that your breeder puts all of his or her guarantees in writing. A responsible breeder will be a source of support throughout your Bulldog's life.

CHAPTER FOUR

Home, Sweet Home

You wouldn't think of having a baby and then bringing him or her home to an empty nursery, right? The same is true when you bring home a new puppy. A Bulldog puppy's immediate needs will be similar to those of a baby: plenty of love and cuddling; a warm, safe environment; more love; nourishing food; plenty of sleep; and still more love and attention. In all likelihood, your new puppy's first time away from his mother and siblings will be the

ride home with you. He's bound to feel a little anxious, so it's your job to make him as comfortable as possible in his new forever home.

PUPPY-PROOFING

Prepare for your new Bulldog by ensuring that your home is a safe and nurturing place for him. The best way to puppy-proof your home is to get down on all fours and look around your house from a puppy's perspective: Don't those electrical cords look tempting? Is that houseplant low enough to pull off the counter? Can you fit a paw into the kitchen trash can?

After your initial puppy-proofing sweep, you still need to keep an eye out for dangerous things around your home that may pose a safety hazard for your growing Bulldog. You will be surprised and amazed by the things your dog can reach, squeeze through, and get into. The key is to be safe from the start, and anticipate mishaps before your puppy misbehaves or gets hurt!

Electrical Cords

Puppies like to chew and need to chew to facilitate healthy teeth and gum development. Especially appealing as chew toys are objects that are somewhat pliable: sturdy rubber toys, human noses, and electrical cords. The first is preferable; the second, a little painful; and the third, disastrous. Your puppy won't know that dangerous wiring

Your curious Bulldog will explore everything he can get his nose into. Always keep an eye on your puppy as he discovers his way around the house and backyard.

A PIECE OF HISTORY

The two dogs that are considered to be the foundation of the modern Bulldog are Crib and Rosa. Illustrated in a painting dated 1817, the dogs have long tails, are much higher on leg than the present Bulldog and do not have the short-muzzled face for which the Bulldog is so well-known.

Name That Bulldog

Choosing a name for your Bulldog is no longer a simple choice of "Winston" or "Churchill." The name you choose says as much about you as it does about your dog. Take your time and choose carefully; you'll be using that name well over 30,000 times during your dog's life! Some names may sound great and unique, but often there is a hidden meaning that carries a negative connotation. "Bruiser" may sound like the perfect name for a bulky male Bulldog, but is it really in keeping with the soft marshmallow personality recognized and loved by all Bulldog fanciers?

While it's a good idea to keep dog names short (one or two syllables), be careful not to select a name that sounds like a cue. Naming your Bulldog "Kit" or "Fay" may be problematic when you start teaching "sit" and "stay." Remember that dogs rely on vocal intonation to interpret our communication. Similarly, avoid choosing a name that sounds like another family member's name, human or animal.

lurks beneath the chewy plastic casing of an electrical cord. The wire can injure the soft tissue of his mouth or, even worse, cause internal injuries if he swallows any of it. And let's not even think about what can happen if a puppy gnaws his way through a live wire.

You can secure electrical cords without sacrificing the convenience of your appliances and lamps. Where possible, run cords underneath carpet or rugs to minimize accessibility. If the appliance is against a wall, gather the excess cord together with a rubber band or twist-tie, and hide it behind the appliance.

If there's simply no way to avoid a loose length of cord, secure it in a length of hard plastic tubing, available at hardware stores. While not impenetrable, it's one more barrier a persistent puppy faces in the search for a chewable object. Another option is to secure excess cords against a baseboard with large staples. Even an inquisitive puppy isn't likely to dedicate himself to prying the cord loose; he isn't even likely to notice it's there.

Of course, you should supervise your puppy at all times and remain fully aware of what he is getting into. But, as with children, puppies can get into trouble in the blink of an eye. When you can't watch him closely, it's best to crate him with an approved chew toy to keep him busy.

Poisonous Substances and Toxic Houseplants

Just as you would secure storage cabinets against a toddler's prying fingers, you want to make sure that all hazardous ingestibles are safely out of your puppy's reach. Do a walk-through of your home, including the garage. Remove all candles and plug-in or solid air-freshening products that are puppy-accessible. Remove

Don't give your puppy free reign of the house right away. Use baby gates and X-pens to block off rooms until your Bulldog becomes more reliable in his surroundings.

candy or nut dishes, especially those that hold chocolate, which is toxic for dogs. Same goes for tobacco products. Even if your new Bulldog pup can't yet reach the pack of cigarettes on the coffee table, he will soon enough. Get in the habit of keeping them somewhere else. Or better yet, kick the habit! Second-hand smoke is bad for anyone, but even more so for your Bulldog because of his sensitive respiratory issues.

Many varieties of common houseplants and flowers, such as poinsettias and chrysanthemums, pose a toxic threat to dogs. Ask the vet or do an internet search to find out if your decorative plants are dangerous, and if so, put them out of your Bulldog's reach.

The Bathroom and Kitchen

In the bathroom, store toothpaste, mouthwash, soaps, colognes, and cleaning products out of reach. Do not use drop-in toilet-bowl cleaners—if your Bulldog drinks out of the toilet, the treated water will poison him. Better still, keep the toilet lid down at all times.

In the kitchen, safely store all sharp objects, foodstuffs, and chemicals. Even though a Bulldog can't reach a kitchen counter with the ease of a Boxer or Lab, it's best not to take the chance. At best, he'll get a whopper of a stomachache from feasting on forbidden fruit; at worst, he can ingest human food that's life-threatening for dogs.

The Garage

The average garage is far too dangerous a place for any dog that isn't scrupulously supervised. Sharp implements, tools, lawn and car chemicals, and even gas fumes spell disaster for a curious puppy. One of the most dangerous substances, anti-freeze, poses a threat even in tiny amounts leaked onto the floor. Antifreeze has a sweet taste appealing to dogs but, when ingested, can kill them.

Some dog owners who don't want "inside dogs" feel that the garage is a viable alternative to living outdoors all the time. Subject to temperature extremes that can be extremely dangerous for your Bulldog, garages are completely unac-ceptable as living space. Moreover, dogs are social animals that thrive on the companionship of their humans. If you don't want a Bulldog to live inside your home as a member of the family, don't get one. Reconsider whether your lifestyle is suited to having a dog at all.

The Yard

A spacious backyard is the perfect place for your Bulldog puppy to explore all the wondrous scents and textures nature has to offer (under your watchful eye, of course). However, the yard has its own hazards that need to be addressed before you bring your puppy home. Make sure that all fencing surrounding the yard is secure and safe for your Bulldog.

Puppies will chew and eat everything from twigs to insects. Certain plants, when ingested, can be poisonous. Unfortunately, some of these are commonly found in our homes and yards, like the attractive rhododendron bush. Wild

Consider the Microchip

In addition to a dog collar and ID tag, think about having your veterinarian insert a microchip in your dog to help find him if he ever gets lost. When scanned, the microchip will show your dog's unique microchip number so that your Bulldog can be returned to you as soon as possible. Go to www .akccar.org to learn more about the nonprofit American Kennel Club Companion Animal Recovery (AKC CAR) pet recovery system.

Since 1995, the AKC CAR recovery service has been selected by millions of dog owners who are grateful for the peace of mind and service that AKC CAR offers. Learn more at www.akccar.org.

AMERICAN KENNEL CLUB™

plants such as bachelor's button and buttercup are also dangerous. Take inventory of the flora in your yard and get rid of anything harmful to your Bulldog.

WHAT TO BUY

It makes a lot of sense to purchase some basic dog supplies before you bring your puppy home. Not only does this preparation save you the stress and inconvenience of not having the necessities on hand when you need them, but you can designate your Bulldog's special eating and resting areas. If you aren't sure where the most convenient locations will be for his food and water bowls, try a few different arrangements before your puppy arrives to see what suits you the best. Once your puppy comes home, consistency will help him learn the lay of his new home and speed up his adjustment to new surroundings.

Collar and Leash

A buckle collar with the puppy's ID tag and a lightweight leash is all that the Bulldog puppy will need at first for outdoor activities. As he grows larger and stronger, he will need a thicker, stronger leash as well.

It's natural for your puppy to chew on anything and everything he can find. Provide lots of different chew toys as an alternative to your furniture.

Dishes

Dog bowls and dishes are typically made of plastic, ceramic, or stainless steel, each with its pros and cons. Plastic bowls are lightweight and easy to clean, but they are chewable and can harbor bacteria if not cleaned thoroughly. Ceramic bowls are decorative and stay put while the enthusiastic eater is chowing down, but they can break easily. You also have to be careful that the pottery hasn't been treated with any kind of hazardous glaze or finish. Stainless steel bowls are unbreakable, unchewable, and easy to clean, making them a logical choice.

Toys

Bulldogs need strong toys when they're puppies and adults. Chew toys are a must, especially when your Bulldog is teething. Make sure toys are durable, made of nontoxic material, and sized appropriately. Toys should not be so small that your pup could choke on them, but not so large that he can't get his small mouth around them. Squeaky toys are always puppy-pleasers, but supervise playtime with them. The soft material encasing the squeaker can be torn apart, and the squeaker itself is a choking hazard. Replace toys as they are damaged.

Increase the size of the toys as your dog grows, making sure that they do not have pieces that can be chewed off and swallowed. Stuffed cloth toys should be made entirely of fabric, without buttons or other ornamentation that pose choking hazards. Strong nylon and hard rubber bones are good choices, too. Rawhide chew toys are popular, but come with their own set of dangers. Indigestible pieces of rawhide can cause intestinal blockage and require surgery, as well as pose a choking threat. Keeping your Bulldog occupied with fun, safe toys will enhance his development and keep him engaged when you're out.

Don't forget the backyard! Make sure that all toxic plants and lawn equipment are stashed safely out of your puppy's reach.

Grooming Equipment

A soft-bristle brush and nail clippers are essential for all puppies, as well as wash-cloths and cotton wipes for cleaning his ears, eyes, and wrinkles. Other necessities include dog shampoo, a dog toothbrush, and dog toothpaste.

Wire Pen and/or Baby Gates

Called an "X-pen," a wire pen is helpful for confining your pup in a larger area than his crate. Likewise, baby gates can block doorways to keep the puppy in a designated puppy-proofed room or area.

Crate and Bedding

Another crucial item to have for your Bulldog is a crate. Some people think a crate represents incarceration, but a responsible dog owner knows that a comfy crate is a haven for his or her Bulldog. All dogs have a strong den instinct that makes them seek out the security of a private space. If there is a lot of activity in your home, your Bulldog will appreciate having a place to get away from it all.

The crate is also an indispensable tool for house-training. Dogs instinctively don't like to soil their sleeping areas, so they will quickly become motivated to wait until they can go outside.

Similarly, the crate is a safe place for your puppy when you can't closely supervise him. This goes for daytime intervals as well as overnight. A puppy can get into mischief the instant your eyes are diverted, mischief that can be dangerous for him as well as destructive for your home.

For successful crate-training, make the crate a cozy space that your Bulldog enjoys. Line the bottom of the crate with newspapers to absorb accidents and top with a soft fleece pad or towel (machine washable, of course). Toss in a small chew toy or fleecy toy, and your Bulldog's "room" is complete. Place the crate near the family's main living area where he can see and hear you nearby, but away from heavy foot traffic and noise. Leave the crate door open so he can go in

Bulldogs are very social and need lots of interaction and playtime. If you work long hours, arrange for a family member, dog walker, or neighbor to visit your Bulldog during the day.

Rotate Toys

It may be tempting to give your puppy all of his toys at once, but don't. Only give him two or three toys at a time to play with, and rotate them with new toys every week or so. Every time you swap out the toys, your puppy will feel like he is getting something new and exciting to play with. Keep toys fun for longer periods of time by rotating them!

and out as he pleases. Later you can work on training him to happily stay in his closed crate while you're away.

INTRODUCTIONS AND INTERACTIONS

Even a well-socialized Bulldog puppy or adult will need time to acclimate to his new house and family members, human or otherwise. It is important that you handle introductions and subsequent interactions with respect for all involved.

Children

A good deal of your Bulldog's playtime will be with your children. It's a good idea to bring your children with you when you visit your puppy's breeder to meet your new pet on his home turf. The physical move to your home will be a major upheaval in your pup's narrow realm of experience, so familiarizing him with the entire family's scents can ease the transition.

A Bulldog's build can handle the rough-and-tumble play children favor. It's important, though, to supervise all interaction between kids and dogs. Instruct children never to tease or bother a dog when he's eating or startle him when he's sleeping, two situations that can easily evoke instinctive aggression. Very young children must be taught to play gently. Toddlers just learning to pet a dog can't distinguish between a gentle pat and a hearty whack. Excited kids may tend to overwhelm a new puppy; they must learn patience and restraint during the pup's adjustment phase. It's your responsibility to make sure everybody knows the rules and how to interact safely with your new Bulldog puppy.

Always supervise unsteady toddlers who are easily knocked over, and infants who emit high-pitched sounds and make sudden movements that arouse a dog's predatory instincts. Better still, don't add a Bulldog to your family until your children are at least seven or eight years old—old enough to understand the boundaries and how to gently interact with a Bulldog.

Do You Need a License?

Other Pets

Bulldogs generally get along fine with other dogs, but it's smart for the multi-pet family to follow a few guidelines. As a rule of thumb, it's better to add a dog of the opposite sex to the one you already have. Same-sex dogs, even females, can become very competitive for dominance, and fights can erupt. Territoriality is a big issue for dogs, so introduce them on neutral territory. Spaying and neutering help diffuse dominance instincts, but it's still preferable to mix sexes. If two dogs decide they dislike each other, the enmity can be permanent. They may have to live separately within the same home.

Cats and Bulldogs get along well if they are raised together. Gradually introduce the two by first putting the cat in a room and closing the door. Let the puppy and cat sniff each other through the crack under the door. Put the puppy in his crate or exercise pen before you let the cat out. Encourage the cat to sniff around the crate or pen at her own pace. If both animals are let loose right away, the cat may feel threatened and run away, inciting the puppy to give chase. Repeat the introduction process as often as necessary until both animals are comfortable around each other. When you think they're ready for a full-out meeting, hold the puppy in your arms for the initial nose-sniffing hello. If all goes well, put the puppy down so the two can interact. Never leave them alone together until you're certain of their friendship, and teach the puppy never to bother the cat when she's eating or using the litter box.

THE FIRST FEW DAYS

The first day or two for your puppy should be fairly quiet. Give him time to get used to his new home, surroundings, and family members. The first night, he may cry a bit; but if you received a blanket from the breeder that has the scent of his mother and littermates, place it in his crate or sleeping area to give him some warmth and security. Remember, he has been uprooted from his littermates, his mother, and his familiar breeder. He will need a day or two to get used to his new

family. If he should cry during the first few nights, let him be. He will eventually quiet down and sleep. By the third night, he should be settled in. Have patience and, within a week or so, it will seem that you, your family, and your puppy have all been together for years.

Routine is very important for a puppy; start him on a feeding schedule from day one. This will help in the house-training regimen as well. Your young puppy will need to be fed four times a day, to start. As he grows, you will eventually cut his meals to two times a day, in the morning and in the evening. Avoid feeding table scraps and keep in mind that certain "people foods," like chocolate, nuts, raisins, grapes, and onions, are toxic to dogs. Do not let your young Bulldog become a fat puppy! Remember that the more active the dog, the more calories he will need. Always have fresh drinking water available; this should include a bowl of water in the house and another outside in the yard, and remember to change the water often.

It's easy to overwhelm your Bulldog puppy with too many new experiences all at once. Give him some alone time to relax and sleep at least a few times a day.

A GREAT START

You are off to an excellent start with your puppy. He will settle in and, as the days go by, you will figure out the additional items that you need. For example, as your puppy learns how to walk on a leash politely, get a longer, possibly retractable, leash for walks around the neighborhood or in the park. You may also want to invest in a dog bed once you think your pup won't chew it up or make a puddle on it. These items can be acquired as needed from your local pet-supply store.

Every day that goes by with your new pup will be a learning experience. Embrace it and treasure it, for these are the memories you will look back on with laughter and sometimes frustration, but always with love. Welcome home, pup!

At a Glance ...

Before your pup comes home, prepare your house with necessary puppy supplies and puppy-proof the home for your clever Bulldog. Puppy kibble, food and water bowls, a collar and leash, ID tags, grooming supplies, and a crate are among the items you will need right away.

Puppy-proof your home by crawling around the house on all fours, viewing the environment from a puppy's perspective. Tie up and hide away all loose electrical cords and items you want to keep away from your puppy's pesky paws and gnawing teeth. Be cognizant of poisonous substances around the house that pose a danger to your curious pup.

All family members should be prepared for the puppy's homecoming, making sure his arrival is low-key and soothing. Your puppy's first experiences outside of the breeder's home should be as calm and comfortable as possible.

Start your Bulldog puppy on a routine as soon as he comes home. The sooner you begin, the sooner he will learn.

CHAPTER FIVE

Build a Training Foundation

Even if you do not plan to compete in conformation or other sporting activities, you still need to train your Bulldog for his happy and safe coexistence with you. This includes house-training, crate-training, and obedience training. Done properly and with love, training is a rewarding experience.

Start training on day one when you bring your Bulldog home from the breeder. Training is all about communicating with your dog. The first

Doggy Day Care

If your family is busy and no one is at home during the day to keep him company, your Bulldog will get pretty bored. If this sounds like your family's weekly routine, you may want to enroll your Bulldog in doggy day care. There are many doggy day care facilities popping up all over the country, and they are a great way to help care for your Bulldog while you are away from the house all day. To find a day care near you, search online at www.dogchannel.com for tips on how to locate a good facility.

step in training is to get to know your pup and his habits, and let your pup get to know you and your habits. With time and patience, you and your pup will learn what makes the other tick, and soon your Bulldog will start to learn and accept what is expected of him—and more importantly, what makes you happy!

WHAT'S YOUR NAME?

A very important factor in training a young pup is to give him a name. Sometimes it may take a week or so before you find a name that fits your dog; other times, you will have him named before you even bring him home. In general, short one- or two-syllable names are the easiest for training, such as "No, Sam." It becomes more difficult when you have to say, "No, Russell John" or "Sit, Mary Beth Rose." You want a name that not only fits your dog's personality but also fits the breed itself. Popular names for Bulldogs are Bella, Tank, Lola, and Mugsy. Use his name often, popping him a treat when he looks at you, and your dog will quickly learn his name.

STAY POSITIVE

Dogs are pack animals; as such, they need a leader. Your Bulldog's first boss was his mother, and all of his life lessons came from her and his littermates. Now you have to assume the role of leader and communicate appropriate behavior in terms that his canine mind will understand. Remember that from his perspective, human rules make no sense at all.

The first twenty weeks of any dog's life is the most valuable learning time, a period when his mind is best able to soak up every lesson, both positive and negative. Do you want a well-behaved Bulldog or an uncontrolled troublemaker? Positive experiences and proper socialization during this period are critical to his future development and stability.

Canine behaviorists and trainers tell us that any behavior that is rewarded will be repeated. This is called positive reinforcement. If something good happens when your puppy does something (like receiving a tasty treat or hugs and kisses) he will naturally want to repeat the behavior. Never underestimate the power of positive reinforcement!

Have treats on hand and be prepared to reinforce good behavior whenever it occurs. That same principle also applies to undesirable behavior, like digging in the trash can, which your dog or puppy does not know is "bad." It's imperative to keep a sharp eye on your puppy so that you can catch him in the act and show him what's expected. By showing him what behaviors are wrong, and popping him a treat when he stops the undesirable behavior by coming to you or sitting politely, he learns what is "bad" and that being good has its rewards.

THE KEYS TO SUCCESS

It will take time for your Bulldog to learn what you expect of him. The first step is to learn how to effectively communicate with your Bulldog. Your dog obviously can't speak your language—and you can't speak his language! You need to learn to communicate with your pup through your tone of voice, simple cues, facial expressions, and hand gestures. With consistency and repetition, your Bulldog will soon get the hang of things—and so will you.

Repetition: The first rule of puppy training is to repeat, repeat, repeat! If your puppy doesn't seem to grasp something, stop for the day, and try again tomorrow. In time, your puppy will understand what you are trying to tell him.

Consistency: Be consistent in everything you do with your Bulldog; puppies thrive on routine. Be especially consistent with your training. Use the same words and phrases for each lesson you teach, and be sure that all of your family members follow your rules for training. Don't let your puppy jump up on the couch one week and forbid it the next! This will only confuse your Bulldog and make training more difficult.

Keep it simple: Remember, you are trying to communicate with your puppy in the clearest way possible. Keep your lessons simple and short. Don't overwhelm him with too much information at once. Training sessions should be no more than five minutes at first, and your training phrases should only be one or two words at most. Be sure that your puppy understands you before you move on to the next lesson.

Watch your tone: Your Bulldog may not understand your words right away, but he does understand the tone of your voice. Keep your training voice light and excited to keep your puppy's attention focused on you. Your dog only wants to please you, and if he hears happiness in your voice and sees it in your face, he will want to repeat whatever he did that made you so happy. Conversely, if your puppy has done something wrong, use a low, serious tone to convey your

Did You Know?

Bulldogs were originally bred in the British Isles as fierce fighting dogs. Today, Bulldogs are known for their loving and gentle temperament.

displeasure. There is no need to yell at your puppy; a low, firm voice is all you need to let your puppy know that he did something wrong.

In the moment: If your Bulldog does something wrong, you need to catch him in the act to show him what is expected. If you don't, there is no use in scolding your pup because he won't understand why he's in trouble. Use the five-second rule: If your Bulldog did something wrong more than five seconds before you notice it, forget about it. Simply vow to catch him in the act the next time.

Don't get frustrated: No matter how angry or frustrated you feel, never, ever hit your puppy or physically correct him in any way. Your relationship with your dog is based on mutual respect. If you disrespect your puppy by hitting him or screaming at him, he will only learn to fear you, which will breed unhappiness, anxiety, and even aggression in your dog. If you feel yourself getting frustrated, take a deep breath and a break. Remember that your puppy is still learning, and he may need a little extra patience and time to understand what you are trying to communicate.

CLICKER TRAINING

A popular method of obedience training is clicker training. First utilized by dolphin trainers, this method of positive reinforcement uses a clicking noise to elicit a certain behavior. A clicker is a small handheld training tool that emits a clicking sound when pressed. As soon as your Bulldog does what he's supposed to, mark the behavior with a click and follow it immediately with a treat. He will soon learn that the clicker sound means that a reward is coming, and that he can prompt you to make that clicker noise by repeating the marked behavior. Because the clicker noise is unlike any other in the dog's everyday environment, it encourages him to focus on the task at hand.

SOCIALIZATION

Introducing your Bulldog to all the sights, sounds, and inhabitants of the world he occupies is an important first step on the road to obedience training. Proper socialization during the first five months exposes him to new people and situations that he is likely to encounter during his everyday life. It also helps prevent extreme shyness or fear. This doesn't mean it's a good idea to take your Bulldog to the Fourth of July fireworks display, but it does mean you should take him with you to as many places to meet as many different people and pets as possible. Allow him to interact, under your supervision, with people of all sizes, genders, and races. Introduce him to people in wheelchairs or on crutches. Let him mingle with other people's pets in a controlled, safe environment. When it comes to socializing your Bulldog, familiarity doesn't breed contempt—it breeds security and self-confidence.

Keep your training sessions short and simple. Quick, repetitive lessons keep training fun and exciting.

It's a Wild World!

Unexpected noises or unusual experiences can scare a puppy. If he develops fear toward a particular sound or activity, it may stick with him for life. To prevent your Bulldog from becoming a scaredy-cat, expose him to a variety of potentially frightening things.

IN THE HOUSE:

- A cookie sheet being dropped on the floor
- The sight and sound of a rolling ball
- A plastic garbage bag snapping open
- A paper bag being crumpled
- A broom and mop in use
- Children's toys, especially those that make noise
- The roar of the vacuum cleaner
- The phone ringing
- The sounds of a dishwasher and garbage disposal in use
- The tumbling noises of the washing machine and dryer

OUTSIDE:

- A revving car engine
- A garbage truck in front of the house
- A motorcycle zipping by
- Kids on bikes, skateboards, and rollerblades

IN THE BACKYARD:

- The lawn mower
- A weed whacker and leaf blower
- A rake or other tools
- Metal and plastic trash cans, including the lids

IN ADDITION, HELP HIM WITH:

- Walking up and down stairs
- Walking over a wooden footbridge
- Walking over a manhole cover
- Riding on an elevator
- Walking on different surfaces, including carpet, artificial turf, slippery floors, and rubber mats

Familiarize your puppy with his name as soon as you bring him home. Teaching him to come when called is an important lesson.

Make Your Puppy a S.T.A.R.

The American Kennel Club has a great program for new puppy owners called the S.T.A.R. Puppy® Program, which is dedicated to rewarding puppies that get off to a good start by completing a basic training class. S.T.A.R. stands for: Socialization, Training, Activity, and Responsibility.

You must enroll in a six-week puppy training course with an AKC-approved evaluator. When the class is finished, the evaluator will test your puppy on all the training taught during the course, such as being free of aggression toward people and other puppies in the class, tolerating a collar or body harness, allowing his owner to take away a treat or toy, and sitting and coming on command.

If your puppy passes the test, he will receive a certificate and a medal. You and your puppy will also be listed in the AKC S.T.A.R. Puppy records. To learn more about the AKC S.T.A.R. Puppy Program or to find an approved evaluator near you, check out www.akc.org/starpuppy.

PUPPY KINDERGARTEN

Another precursor to formal obedience training is a puppy socialization class, sometimes known as "puppy kindergarten." This is where puppies get together in a controlled setting and learn how to interact with dogs other than their littermates. This reinforces pack behavior, as the puppies learn what is and is not acceptable among other dogs. It also enables the trainer leading the class to see if any puppy exhibits unusually aggressive behavior toward other dogs. Puppy kindergarten sets the stage for obedience training and offers you the expertise and advice of a professional.

It's important to find the right obedience class and trainer before you enroll your Bulldog. Ask your vet, breeder, local pet store, breed club, or dog-owning friends for referrals. Once you get some names, schedule a visit to the training center with your dog to meet the trainer, see the facilities, and find out the methods of training used in the classes.

Puppy kindergarten is also where your puppy will actively use a collar and leash for the first time. It's best to familiarize your Bulldog with both before starting classes. Your pup may already be comfortable with his collar, but a leash will be entirely new. Keep in mind that he has no clue what this long thing is that you've attached to the strange thing around his neck. Puppy kindergarten will show both of you how to walk properly on a leash, as well as a few other simple cues. The sooner you let your Bulldog puppy know what you expect of him, the faster he will learn how to function as a member of your family.

PUPPY PLAYTIME

If you decide to wait until your puppy is a little older before getting serious about obedience training, you can still start training him without his even knowing. Play these games with your puppy and instill in him the focus and foundation needed for further training.

Come, Bulldog, Come!

This is a fun game to play between two people, and it will help your puppy learn his name and to come when you call him. Sit on the floor on one side of a room, and have a friend or family member sit opposite you a short distance away. Place your puppy in the middle of the room. Call to your puppy, saying his name in a happy voice, and clap your hands. Get excited and say, "Come, puppy, come!" Your Bulldog should run toward you excitedly. When he gets to you, praise him and pet him. Now it's your friend's turn. Have your friend call your puppy in the same way, using his name, "Come, puppy, come!" After a few days, your puppy will learn to come when called, and he'll start to recognize his name. Eventually, you can add a tennis ball to the game and toss it between the two of you. Reward the pup for picking up the ball and releasing it to the nearest person.

Hide-and-Seek

Another game to help your puppy learn to come is a simple game of hide-and-seek. You can play this inside or outside, just be sure you are in a safely confined area. When your Bulldog is distracted, quickly bend down behind a nearby bush

Who's the Boss?

Wild dogs live in groups called "packs." In packs, one dog acts as the leader and all the other dogs follow him and learn from him. Although your Bulldog isn't wild, he still needs to have a leader. By training your dog when he is a puppy, he will learn that you are the pack leader and to follow your instructions.

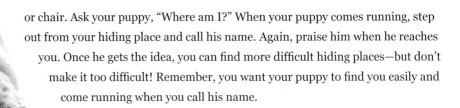

or chair. Ask your puppy, "Where am I?" When your puppy comes running, step out from your hiding place and call his name. Again, praise him when he reaches you. Once he gets the idea, you can find more difficult hiding places—but don't make it too difficult! Remember, you want your puppy to find you easily and come running when you call his name.

Find Your Toy

This is a great game to help your puppy refine his scenting skills. Pick out one of your Bulldog's favorite toys and place it in the middle of the room in front of your pup. Ask, in a sprightly voice, "Where's your toy?" and coax him to run and pick it up. Praise him with lots of pets and

Body Language

Your Bulldog doesn't speak English, but he does have a language all his own. Dogs communicate mostly through body language. The most common canine body postures convey emotional responses to the environment, to other dogs, and to humans. Here are just a few body postures to keep an eye out for in your Bulldog:

Greeting: Most dogs will approach one another cautiously. The dominant of the two dogs will hold his head, ears, and tail high, and the more submissive of the two will crouch low and hold his ears back and tail down. Both will sniff one another, smelling each other's unique scent.

Play bow: When your Bulldog wants to play, he'll crouch down on his front legs and hold his rump high in the air, wagging his hindquarters back and forth. With ears up, mouth relaxed, and tongue out, you can't mistake this stance for anything but excitement and eagerness to play.

Defensive aggression: If a Bulldog feels threatened, his hackles will rise and he will shift his weight to his rear legs. His mouth and face will be tense, and he may growl and flash his teeth. Beware of a dog in this position, as attack may soon follow.

Submission: A submissive Bulldog will either lower his head and hindquarters, pull his ears back, and half-close his eyes, or he will lay on his back and expose his belly. Either way, your Bulldog is showing you that he is surrendering to a dominant animal, whether dog or human.

belly rubs. After he gets used to the idea, move the toy under a couch cushion or blanket so that only a part of it shows. Again, ask your puppy, "Where's your toy?" After he's found his toy a few times, you can hide the toy completely, letting your Bulldog use his nose to find it. You'll be surprised at how quickly and easily he will.

Roughhouse

Act like a puppy! Get on all fours and gently wrestle with your puppy. This is a great way to have fun with your Bulldog and teach him how to play gently with a human. If he gets overexcited and nips at your hands, firmly say "Ouch!" and pull away. Wait until your puppy is relaxed again to resume playing. This light roughhousing helps your puppy learn what is acceptable when playing with a human and helps develop your communication skills through body language and expression.

WITH FLYING COLORS

Once you and your puppy complete a puppy kindergarten course, and you feel that your Bulldog is ready for the next step in training, move on to more advanced training courses. Get in touch with your local breed club, the Bulldog Club of America (www.thebca.org), or the American Kennel Club (www.akc.org) and find out all the options for you and your Bulldog.

Knowing whether you want to get involved in conformation, obedience, therapy work, or any other activities will help you decide what method of training to pursue next. In any case, remember that dog training is a lifetime pursuit. The more you train your Bulldog, the stronger your bond will be with your dog.

Be consistent with your puppy. Don't snuggle with him on the couch one day but scold him for jumping on the cushions the next.

At a Glance ...

Positive training is the most effective method of dog training. Ignore bad behavior and reward good behavior with lots of love and praise, and soon your puppy will learn to follow your cues. Never use physical force with your puppy or punish him. Negative reinforcement only breeds fear and aggression in a dog.

· ·

Socialization is very important for your puppy during the first five months of his life. This impressionable time is when your puppy will come to recognize the world and grow comfortable with the people in it. Introduce your Bulldog to as many new and different people and places as you can, and keep all of his experiences friendly and calm.

· ·

Enroll your puppy in a puppy kindergarten class as soon as possible. This early training course is a way to socialize your Bulldog with other puppies in a controlled environment and to discuss training techniques with and seek advice from a professional trainer.

· ·

Dog training is a lifetime pursuit. Never stop training your Bulldog. In time, with patience and consistency, positive training will strengthen the bond with your dog and allow you to participate in a variety of activities.

Proper Potty Principles

The first order of business when you bring a puppy home is to teach him where it's appropriate to do his business. Even if your Bulldog puppy is a quick learner, don't expect potty perfection right away. His immature bladder can't hold out as long as his will can; accidents will happen. House-training requires patience and commitment, so be prepared to revolve your daily routine around this training task for a few weeks or longer.

When you take your puppy outside to go potty, do not distract him with play until he has done his business.

INSIDE OR OUTSIDE

Before you start house-training, first decide what method you are going to use. Take a look at your home and living environment. Is it difficult to quickly reach an outside area where your puppy can relieve himself? Will your dog be confined within your home for long periods of time during the day without access to a backyard? Do you live in a high-rise apartment that is a long way from a bathroom spot for your pup? If any of the answers to these questions is yes, you may want to consider training your puppy to relieve himself on newspaper or a puppy pad in your home. Keep in mind, however, that if you eventually want your puppy to relieve himself outside, it's best not to paper-train him first because it will confuse him when you try to retrain him to go outside. Pick a method and stick to it.

If you decide that paper-training is best for your lifestyle, the best way to train your puppy is to confine him to a small area or room using baby gates or X-pens. Cover the entire floor of the area with newspapers or puppy pads. Place your dog's crate and food and water to one side of the area, leaving the puppy plenty of room

A PIECE OF HISTORY

Although originated in England, the Bulldog has been a popular breed in the United States since the turn of the century. Even two U.S. presidents owned Bulldogs: Warren Harding owned a Bulldog called Oh Boy, and Calvin Coolidge had a Bulldog named Boston Beans.

When your Bulldog is older, you can let him outside alone in a fenced yard to go to the bathroom. He'll let you know when he's done and wants to come back inside.

to go to the bathroom on the opposite side. Put a few toys in as well so that your puppy feels comfortable in his retreat. Whenever you cannot watch your puppy, place him in this area. After a day or two, you'll notice that your puppy will start to go to the bathroom in one general area. Each day, remove a section of newspaper or padding. After a couple of weeks, your puppy will relieve himself consistently on one or two pieces of newspaper or padding. If he has an accident off the paper, just add a piece of paper back until he starts going on the paper once more. Soon, your puppy will understand that the paper is where he should relieve himself.

THE SWEET SPOT

If you decide that you want your puppy to go potty outside from the start, first identify the outdoor area you want to designate as your Bulldog's bathroom. You can anticipate certain times when your puppy will need to eliminate, such as after a meal or upon waking from a nap. Immediately take the pup to his outside spot and encourage him to go. Be patient; this can take up to twenty minutes, as all the fascinating new smells outside will distract him from emptying his bladder. It's important to keep an eye out so you can praise and reward your Bulldog immediately after. Rewarding him even a few minutes too late will not work because your puppy won't connect the reward with the action.

You will soon learn the habits of your dog. It is essential to take your puppy out when he gets up in the morning, after he eats, before he goes to bed, after long naps, and any time he looks like he's sniffing out a place to "go." A young puppy may need more than ten potty trips a day, but most adult dogs will only have to be taken out three or four times a day. Some dogs will go to the door and bark when they want to be let out, and others will nervously circle around. Watch and learn your Bulldog's signs, and don't ignore the signals he gives you.

Routine, consistency, and an eagle eye are your keys to house-training success. Always lead your puppy on his leash outside to the same area, telling him "outside" as you go out. If you have a fenced yard, eventually you will be able to let the pup out alone and he will find the spot on his own.

Pick a "potty" word or phrase (like "hurry up," "go potty," or "get busy") and use it every time he does his business, lavishing "good puppy!" praise on him afterward. Use the same exit door for every potty trip, and confine your puppy to the exit area so he can find it when he needs it. Again, don't ignore his signals! Don't allow him to roam the house until he's completely house-trained; how will he find that outside door if he's three or four rooms away?

CRATE-TRAINING

Crates are a major help in house-training, as most dogs do not want to dirty their living quarters. The crate is actually a multipurpose dog accessory: it's your Bulldog's personal doghouse within your home, a humane house-training tool,

Be consistent in your house-training methods from the start. A paper-trained puppy may get confused if you suddenly want him to start going outside.

Three Keys to House-Training

It's nice to have an obedient Bulldog that will sit on cue or even down-stay off leash for sixty seconds, but it's not critical to your daily life. House-training, on the other hand, is critical, and it's at the top of the list of behavior controls that all dog owners must accomplish. Here are the keys to successful potty-training:

CONSISTENCY: Your puppy is relying on you to establish a training routine and stick to it. House-training is only important to you, not the puppy. If you want your puppy to succeed (and you definitely do!), make a real effort to tackle this first training hurdle. Decide on a plan of action for how you want your dog to behave, and stick to it in your training.

REPETITION: Bulldogs are creatures of habit and need to understand what's expected of them. An owner can ingrain what he or she expects by repeating the same cues, and doing the same routine day after day until the puppy responds without failure.

WORD ASSOCIATION: Decide on the words you will use for house-training, and be consistent. "Do your business," "outside," and "go potty" are three of the most common phrases owners use to communicate with their dogs about when it's time to go.

Vacation Time

a security measure that will protect your household and belongings when you're not home, a travel aid to house and protect your dog when you are traveling (most motels will accept a crated dog), and, finally, a comfy dog space for your puppy when your anti-dog relatives come to visit. Some experienced breeders insist on crate use after their puppies leave, and some even begin to crate-train their pups before they send them to their new homes.

The size of the crate is important—it should be big enough for the dog to sit, stand, and turn around easily inside. Because a puppy will soon outgrow a small crate, most owners prefer to purchase an adult-size crate. However, if you do this, you need to partition off the extra space because your puppy will soil one end of the crate without compromising his sleeping area at the other. This can interfere with house-training progress.

Beyond a useful house-training tool, the crate is a dog's special haven, a personal, protected place where he can rest and relax in security and comfort. Dogs like the secure feeling of a "den," so crate-training is actually in sync with his natural canine instincts.

Reward and treat your puppy as soon as he goes potty so that he connects the praise with relieving himself outside.

DOG MEETS CRATE

Introduce the crate to your puppy as soon as he comes home so he learns that it is his special "house." To show your Bulldog that his crate is his castle, line it with a blanket or fleece pad so the floor is soft and cozy. Throw in a small toy he particularly likes. Entice him inside with a treat, leaving the crate door open while he explores inside. Pick a crate cue, such as "kennel," "inside," or "crate," and use it every time he enters. Praise him while he's inside and allow him to wander in and out at will. He may even decide it's a good place for a nap.

Once your puppy is comfortable with the crate, serve one of his meals inside it with the door open. If he's okay with that, try serving another meal inside the crate with the door closed, but remain where he can see you. When he's finished eating, praise his good behavior and take him outside to eliminate right away.

The next phase involves relocating your Bulldog to his crate the next time he settles down for a nap. Close the crate door, but remain close by where he can hear you and the family. Praise him for being good while crated, but don't take him out if he begins to cry or whimper. This will only teach your puppy that crying gets him what he wants, a behavior you don't want to reinforce. If he starts to cry, simply ignore him. Take him out of the crate only after he settles down. He'll soon understand that good behavior has its rewards. Gradually lengthen the time your dog spends in the crate, always taking him out when he behaves properly, until you've progressed from stepping into the next room for a minute to being

Because you need to take your puppy outside every couple of hours, it's a good idea to set a timer every ninety minutes to remind yourself it's potty time.

Leave No Trace

Your pup will inevitably have a few (or many!) accidents while house-training. Luckily, you can use many household items to help keep your home clean during this training stage.

■ **If you don't have any store-bought cleaners on hand, create your own using ¼ cup of white vinegar to 1 quart of water.**

■ **Salt will absorb fresh urine and remove some of the scent.**

■ **In a pinch, rubbing the area with a dryer sheet can remove some of the odor.**

■ **White toothpaste can sometimes remove some tough stains from carpet. But beware—it can also ruin the carpet's coloring! Never use toothpaste on dark-colored carpets.**

away for ten minutes. Continue to increase the time you're out of sight while he's in the crate until he's content with the whole idea.

Your puppy should sleep in his crate from his very first night. He may whine for the first few nights, but be strong! If you release him when he cries, he learns that if he cries, he gets his way. A better option is to place the crate next to your bed at night for the first few weeks. Your presence will comfort him, and you'll also know if he needs a midnight potty trip. Whatever you do, do not bring the puppy into bed with you. To a dog, being on the bed means equality with his owners, which is not a good idea this early on, as you establish your leadership.

CRATE-TRAINING 101

Once your puppy feels comfortable in his crate, it will become an irreplaceable house-training tool. Because your Bulldog now sees his crate as his personal relaxation and sleeping place, he will instinctively not want to soil it. Use this canine instinct to your house-training advantage. Put the pup in his crate whenever you are not around to watch him, or if you simply need a break from your puppy to take a shower, clean the house, or run some errands. Don't feel bad, if you've introduced the crate properly, your puppy should like spending time in his crate—it gives him a much-needed break from the exciting (and sometimes tiring) world around him. And never fear, he will let you know when he needs to go to the bathroom.

Every time you let your puppy out of his crate, take him outside right away to relieve himself. Say your cue words, "go potty" or "do your business." Don't let your Bulldog get distracted before going to the bathroom. Once he has relieved himself, praise him with lots of clapping and smiles. Now that he's gone to the bathroom, you can give him some free time to roam around the house. Still, don't let your Bulldog out of your sight. Follow him around on his adventures and watch closely should he start to circle or squat to go to the bathroom. If he does, scoop him up quickly and take him immediately to his outside area again. In time, he will realize that outside is where he needs to do his business, and nowhere else!

After some free time and playing, put your puppy back in his crate to relax for an hour or two. Your Bulldog puppy is still a baby, and he needs a lot of time to sleep and process everything he is learning and experiencing. After a few weeks (or a couple of months), your puppy will start to get the idea of house-training. As you gain confidence in your puppy's understanding, give him more

You don't have to play a guessing game when it comes to house-training your Bulldog. A consistent feeding schedule helps regulate your dog's elimination habits.

and more freedom around the house a little bit at a time. If your puppy regresses and has an accident, don't worry, just take a step back and watch your puppy more carefully.

DON'T ABUSE IT

Despite its many benefits, crate use can be abused. Puppies under twelve weeks of age should never be confined for more than two hours at a time, unless, of course, they are sleeping at night. A general rule of thumb is three hours maximum for a three-month-old pup, four to five hours for the four- to five-month-old, and no more than six hours for dogs six months of age and older. If you're not home, arrange for a relative or dogsitter to let him out to exercise and potty.

One final, but important, rule of crate use: never use the crate for punishment. Successful crate-training depends on your puppy's positive association with his "house." If the crate represents punishment, he will resist using it as his safe place. Sure, you can crate your pup after he has sorted through the trash. Just don't do it in an angry fashion or tell him, "Bad dog, crate!"

ACCIDENTS HAPPEN

When an accident does occur indoors, don't scold or punish your Bulldog. Unless you catch him in the act, he won't understand that you're angry about something he did ten minutes ago. Never rub his nose in the mess. This does not teach him

Use the same bathroom cues each time you take your dog outside. Always praise him when he goes, and he'll soon learn what you're asking him to do.

The Attention Seeker

Most Bulldogs will do anything for attention. Clowns to the core, this attention-seeking quality may keep Bulldogs from being able to concentrate on lessons during training sessions. To help center your pup's focus, ignore him for a few minutes before training so that he will be calm and eager for your attention. When you do finally start your training lesson, he will be in the right mind-set for learning what you have to teach.

coming, you want him to stay or come at your command. When the unexpected happens, you need to be prepared.

THE BASICS

The basic cues every dog should learn early in life are *sit*, *stay*, *down*, *come*, *heel*, and *take it* and *leave it*. The intelligent Bulldog should have no difficulty learning these cues as long as you make training fun and rewarding. To get started, slip on his training collar, attach his leash, and fill your pockets with plenty of treats.

Sit

Take a treat in your right hand and bring it to your Bulldog's nose. Let him smell and lick the treat, but do not let him take it. Say "sit" and slowly raise your hand with the treat upward so he is looking toward the sky. His rump will naturally go down to help him keep his balance. At this point, give him the treat and praise him lavishly. Repeat this exercise a few times daily, and within a week or so, your Bulldog will learn that "sit" means sit!

Down

To a dog, the down position is a submissive posture not to be assumed lightly. He must trust you implicitly to go against the instincts that tell him to remain upright and self-confident. It's important that you don't force the down position on your Bulldog, or he may develop a fear that manifests in noncompliance or aggression.

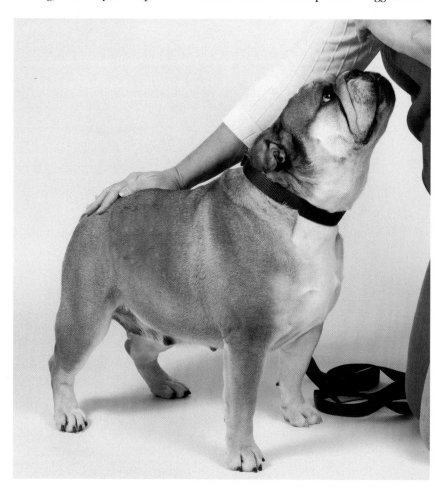

Most dogs naturally sit when they look up at your hand holding a treat. However, some Bulldogs may require a gentle, guiding hand.

Start basic training with the *sit* cue. All dogs learn this cue quickly, which is good because *sit* is the foundation for more difficult cues.

Put your Bulldog in a sit position next to your left leg. Put a food treat in your right hand and hold the leash in the same hand. Gently, with no real pressure, rest your left hand on the dog's back where the shoulders meet. You're not going to push him down, but your hand will serve as a guide.

Put your food hand in front of his nose and softly say "down" as you slowly lower the hand, with its enticing smell, to the floor. When it reaches the floor, slide it along the floor away from the dog while verbally encouraging him saying, "down." Your calm voice will reassure him that he needn't worry about assuming a submissive pose. His forelegs should stretch out as he gravitates toward the treat. When his elbows touch the floor, give him the treat and praise him, still in a calm voice. Encourage him to stay in the down position for a few seconds to reinforce the fact that he's not threatened while in this position.

Stay

The *stay* cue is a logical follow-up to the *sit* and *down* cues. Start with your Bulldog on-leash in a sit position next to your left leg. With a treat inside your right hand, hold it in front of his nose while you step out with your right foot to face

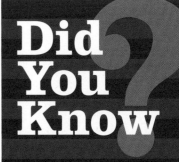

Did You Know?

The first dog show with classes for the Bulldog was held in Birmingham, England in 1860. By 1875, the first Bulldog Club of America National Show was held; this became an annual event that still occurs today.

him, saying "stay." While he's licking and sniffing at the treat in your hand, count to five and resume your position alongside him, then release the treat and praise him. Practice this every day for a week before moving to the next step.

Once your Bulldog understands the premise of *stay*, it's time to increase the distance between you while he's in the stay position. Grasp the leash toward the loop end, giving yourself some extra slack to work with. When you step out to face the dog, say "stay" and put up your hand in front of his face in a stop gesture. The goal is for your dog to learn that he will receive a treat only when you return to his side. Start out right in front of your dog and gradually build up time and distance. When you've reached a distance of 3 feet from your dog for thirty seconds, begin to add more distance and time to the stay. Give your dog lots of praise when he gets it right. The *stay* cue can be a lifesaver in a dangerous situation.

Come

Speaking of important cues, the *come* cue is one that you should present as a fun game, one that your Bulldog will love to play. Any dog will approach or follow you, except in two situations: when you happily call the dog to come to you, but punish him once he arrives; and when you give the *come* cue in a fearful or upset voice. If your Bulldog has done something to displease you, remember that unless you've caught him in the act, you cannot teach him what is expected. Calling him

Bulldogs are smart, so once they have mastered basic obedience, you can teach them tricks like shake hands.

Can Your Dog Pass the Canine Good Citizen® Test?

An AMERICAN KENNEL CLUB Program

Once your Bulldog is ready for advanced training, you can start training him for the American Kennel Club Canine Good Citizen® Program. This program is for dogs that are trained to behave at home, out in the neighborhood, and in the city. It's easy and fun to do. Once your dog learns basic obedience and good canine manners, a CGC evaluator gives your dog ten basic tests. If he passes, he's awarded a Canine Good Citizen® certificate. Many trainers offer classes with the test as the final to graduate from the class. To find an evaluator in your area, go to www.akc.org/events/cgc/cgc_bystate.cfm.

Many therapy dogs and guide dogs are required to pass the Canine Good Citizen® test in order to help as working dogs in the community. There are ten specific tests that a dog must master in order to pass the Canine Good Citizen® test. A well-trained dog will:

1. Let a friendly stranger approach and talk to his owner.
2. Let a friendly stranger pet him.
3. Be comfortable being groomed and examined by a friendly stranger.
4. Walk on a leash and show that he is in control and not overly excited.
5. Move through a crowd politely and confidently.
6. Sit and stay on command.
7. Come when called.
8. Behave calmly around another dog.
9. Not bark at or react to a surprise distraction.
10. Show that he can be left with a trusted person away from his owner.

In order to help your dog pass the AKC CGC test, first enroll him in basic training classes and a CGC training class. You can find classes and trainers near you by searching the AKC website. When you feel that your Bulldog is ready to take the test, locate an AKC-approved CGC evaluator to set up a test date, or sign up for a test that is held at a local AKC dog show or training class. For more information about the AKC Canine Good Citizen® Program, visit the website at www.akc.org/events.cgc.

Walking your dog can be difficult if he pulls on the leash or constantly walks in front of you. Teach your Bulldog to heel with consistent training and positive reinforcement.

to you for a scolding only teaches him that coming to you when called results in bad things. Likewise, if you call to your dog in a distressed tone, he'll conclude that whatever is scaring you is likely to scare him, too. He'll either stay where he is or run in the opposite direction.

Most people find that "come" is not the word that evokes the desired action. The right cue that inspires your Bulldog to come running might be "treat" or "hugs!" It doesn't matter which word or phrase you use, as long as your Bulldog understands that he will receive lots of praise and something yummy when he comes to you as requested.

To practice the *come* cue, start out with your dog on a short leash in the sit position. Step in front of him and hold a treat up in front of you and say "come" as you start walking backward. When your dog gets up and walks forward to take the treat, give him the treat and praise him. Keep practicing this exercise, moving farther and farther away. This will not only teach your Bulldog to come when called, but it will also help you both practice your *sit* and *stay* cues as well.

Heel

Heeling is the action of a dog walking beside his person with an equivalent stride, and automatically assuming a sit when the person stops. The *heel* cue needs to be perfected if you plan to show your Bulldog, but it's also useful for everyday walking, especially if different people walk your dog, such as a dog-sitter or relative. A dog that constantly pulls on the leash may be too much for a youngster or elderly person to handle. At the very least, it's no fun walking such a dog, even if you're in great physical shape.

To teach the *heel* cue, position your Bulldog next to your left side and hold the leash short in your left hand. Your right hand can hold the loop end and excess leash. Say "heel" and step out with your left foot, keeping the dog close to you as you take three paces, then stop and return him to a sit. This may take a few tries, but when he performs, praise him excitedly without touching him. After a minute, say "heel" again and take three steps, stop, and give the *sit* cue. Practice until your Bulldog heels nicely every time you walk him on a leash. Remember to release him from the heel position with an "okay" or "good boy" to indicate that the exercise is finished.

Take It and Leave It

The *take it* and *leave it* cues are important for your Bulldog to learn because there may come a time when your dog will cross something in his path that is not good for him. For example, say you are on a walk and you pass a piece of trash on the ground. Of course, this is unsafe for your Bulldog to eat, but he doesn't know the difference! You want to be able to stop your Bulldog and be sure that he will obey you and leave it when you tell him to.

Stand Up to Distractions

Once your puppy understands the basic cues and can perform them reliably without hesitation, add some distractions to the routine to test how well your Bulldog will perform the lessons in the real world. Take your Bulldog into a room with his favorite toys spread around, or have another member of the family sit nearby and watch. After he masters his cues with these small distractions, up the ante by having the person whistle, clap, or talk loudly around the pup. Train your dog to focus on your directions despite the distractions that may surround him.

A harness is often used with brachyochephalic breeds to lessen the strain on their neck. If your Bulldog seems uncomfortable with a collared leash, try a harness.

To begin, place a treat in the palm of your hand and offer it to your puppy. Say "take it" as he eats the treat. Do this a few times to get your Bulldog used to the phrase and its meaning. After the third or fourth time, when your puppy leans forward to eat the treat, close your fingers around the treat and don't say anything. Be ready for your Bulldog to lick, nuzzle, paw, and cry at your hand for the treat. After a few moments, only after your puppy calms himself and settles down, open your palm and let him take the treat as you say "take it." Keep teaching this lesson for a few days until your puppy consistently waits for your cue to take the treat.

Once your puppy understands (and has the patience) to wait for your cue to take the treat, you can move on to the *leave it* cue. Place a treat in the palm of your hand again, and lower your hand in front of your Bulldog as you say "leave it." When he goes for the treat, say "leave it" again as you close your fingers around the treat. Keep repeating this lesson until he stops going for the treat. When he waits, open your palm and say "take it," letting your Bulldog then take the treat. As always, keep repeating this lesson until your dog consistently waits when you say "leave it" and consistently takes the treat when you say "take it." You can then build up the time between your *take it* and *leave it* cues to solidify his understanding.

Don't be discouraged. This lesson will take some time for your Bulldog to learn. Once he gets the hang of the cues, move the lesson outside into a real-life situation. Place a few toys along your usual walking route. When you approach the toy, if your dog tries to pick it up, say "leave it" in a firm voice and keep moving forward. Praise him lavishly when he leaves the toy alone. Repeat this lesson once or twice on your daily walks and soon your pup will learn that you know what's best for him.

PROBLEM BEHAVIORS

No dog is perfect, but the Bulldog comes close! Nevertheless, your Bulldog puppy may have a few bad habits that need some attention and training guidance. Are you at your wit's end with your dog's barking? Embarrassed by your Bulldog's tendency to jump up and smother your guests with affection? Concerned with your Bulldog's rough, mouthy playing style? You can solve these common problems before they become permanent bad habits with a few simple training techniques.

Chewing

Did you come home to find that your Bulldog has ripped your couch cushions to shreds, or gnawed your favorite shoes to bits? Your puppy chews for comfort because it's a natural and familiar thing to do, but also because it feels good on his growing jaw and baby gums and teeth. The best thing to do is to redirect your Bulldog's chewing to something acceptable. When you catch your pup chewing on something he shouldn't, remove the item and supply an appropriate chew toy instead. If you find him chewing on his chew toy around the house, praise him for his good behavior and reward him with a treat.

If your Bulldog puppy jumps up, you might think it's cute, but when he's fully grown, you won't appreciate being tackled by a 40-pound dog. The best way to stop this behavior is to ignore it.

Mouthing

The Bulldog can be quite a mouthy breed and often conveys his excitement through playful nips and gentle bites on your hands and arms during playtime. It's important to stop this mouthing behavior while your Bulldog puppy is young to avoid a possible biting tendency when he is older.

A puppy uses his mouth to explore the world around him. When your Bulldog was very young, he playfully mouthed and nipped at his mother and siblings, learning exactly how much pressure would hurt them and what type of communication was acceptable among his canine family. Your puppy will use the same mouthing process to learn more about you and the rules of human interaction and communication. When your puppy playfully bites or mouths your hands or arms, say "ouch" or "no bite" and immediately stop playing. This reaction will teach your Bulldog that biting and mouthing is not an acceptable mode of communication with humans.

Jumping Up

Many dogs jump up on people because they cannot contain their excitement. They simply want to let you know that they are happy to see you (or meet you), and they can only do this if they have your attention immediately—by force if necessary! Like most other behaviors, it's important to start training your dog not to jump up while he is a puppy. When you first come home from work or after running errands, ignore your puppy when he jumps up against your leg. Wait until he is calm to greet him. If he persists in jumping, turn away from him, and give him the *sit* cue. When he sits, ignore him for a few moments. Only then should you greet him and praise him for waiting calmly. Practice this with guests when they come over to visit. Soon your Bulldog will learn to be a patient gentleman for both you and your guests.

Barking

Barking is a natural behavior for all dogs; they use their voice to communicate with other dogs. Vocalizing is not always a bad thing, especially if your dog is

Stopping Separation Anxiety

A dog with separation anxiety exhibits extreme behavior problems when left alone. After his owner leaves the house, the dog has a panic response and will dig, chew, or scratch at the door trying to get to his owner. He will howl, cry, and bark, and may even urinate or defecate from distress.

Some things seem to trigger separation anxiety. Dogs that are used to constantly being with their owners but are suddenly left alone for the first time may exhibit panicky behavior. A traumatic event, such as time spent in a shelter or kennel, may also trigger anxiety. A change in the family's routine or structure, such as a child leaving for college, can also cause stress in a dog's life.

If you believe your Bulldog is suffering from separation anxiety, here are some ways to address the problem:

● Keep your departures and arrivals low-key. Quietly leave the house and ignore your dog for a few minutes before acknowledging him when you return.

● Leave your dog with an item of clothing that smells like you.

● If your dog chews excessively when you are gone, leave him with a chew toy filled with treats.

More severe cases of separation anxiety require you to systematically train your dog to get used to being alone. Discuss options with your veterinarian and trainer—they may be able to offer more long-term solutions, such as prescription drugs for separation anxiety that can be used during behavior-modification training.

warning you of a stranger's presence in the house or letting you know he needs to go outside. Keeping that in mind, try to differentiate a warning bark from a frenzied barking episode. If you can target when and why your Bulldog is barking, you will be able to correct or minimize the barking behavior in certain situations.

Does your Bulldog bark incessantly when a stranger walks by the front of the house or when someone knocks at the front door? If so, your dog is a protective barker. He may see these people as threats to his home, or simply be warning you of their presence. If this is the case, invite a friend or neighbor to walk along the sidewalk in front of your house or ring your doorbell. When your Bulldog starts barking, ignore him until he quiets down. When he settles and is calm, give him a treat and lots of praise. Have your friend then repeat the action. Keep doing this until your Bulldog gets the idea.

If your Bulldog barks for no reason when he is bored, chances are you give your dog the attention he craves when he starts needlessly barking. Even yelling at the dog or pointing and shushing your pup is a form of attention, and your Bulldog may realize that he can focus your attention on him simply by barking. Think of it as your dog saying, "Look at me, Mom! I'm here, Dad!" If this describes your dog's barking habits, try a new tactic. Ignore him. This may be difficult at first, especially with a persistent Bulldog, but eventually your dog will give up and quiet down. When he does, give him a treat and praise him. He will eventually learn that you will only give him the attention he wants when he is quiet. If your dog still doesn't get the idea, try putting some coins in an empty aluminum can. When your dog barks, shake the can and firmly say "quiet" only once. This should startle him into silence. Give him some praise. Eventually, he will associate your *quiet* cue with not barking.

One of the most important exercises to teach your dog is to come when called. Praise your dog lavishly when he responds to his name.

Bulldogs in the Community

Passed the AKC Canine Good Citizen® test with ease? Wondering how you can use your Bulldog's talents to help the community? Bulldogs have a natural ability to bring comfort through their sweet, loving demeanors and their hard-to-resist mugs. If you want to share the happiness that your Bulldog brings you every day with those in need, consider training your Bulldog for therapy work. The AKC Therapy Dog Program is a great way to get involved in the community and bring joy to both adults and children in need of a little canine support and cheer. Find out more at www.akc.org/akc therapydog.

Does your Bulldog bark all day when he is home alone? He may be suffering from separation anxiety. Bulldogs are extremely devoted to their owners. As such, they are extremely sad to see you leave. Sometimes, dogs will become so depressed or panicked at your departure that they develop certain destructive or obsessive-compulsive behaviors. Barking is one symptom of separation anxiety.

STILL NEED HELP?

Even the most consistent and responsible owners still may have trouble training their dogs or solving certain problem behaviors. In this case, call a professional dog trainer to help. More importantly, a trainer will provide tips and training techniques that you can use with your dog in the future. No two Bulldogs are the same, and every Bulldog needs a different training approach. A professional trainer will help you find the best approach for your dog.

When looking for a dog trainer, ask for referrals from your vet or breeder, and search the websites of responsible and trusted organizations such as the

Association of Pet Dog Trainers (www.apdt.com) or the Certification Council for Professional Dog Trainers (www.ccpdt.org). You can also contact the Bulldog Club of America (www.thebca.org), which maintains a nationwide directory of trainers. Be sure that your trainer has been certified by the CCPDT. This organization ensures that the trainer has demonstrated his or her abilities and prowess as a dog trainer and makes sure that the trainer is educated in the latest training techniques and equipment.

OBEDIENCE CLASSES

In time, with consistency and repetition, your Bulldog will learn to master all these basic cues and behaviors. To help get you started, enroll in a puppy kindergarten class. Finding a class in your area is easy. Ask your veterinarian, breeder, local pet store, or breed club for a list of puppy training classes near you. They will be happy to provide you with some recommendations.

After your puppy learns the basics, there are many other ways you can continue your dog's training. Seek out an AKC S.T.A.R. Puppy® Program in your area (see page 52), which will give your puppy a great foundation for more advanced training in his adult years. To find out more, visit www.akc.org/starpuppy. If your dog takes to training, the next step would be to sign up for the AKC Canine Good Citizen® Program (see page 73) led by an AKC-certified instructor. With these training classes under your belt, you and your Bulldog can move on to more advanced activities such as obedience, conformation, and even therapy work. The American Kennel Club offers all of these activities and more, which are discussed in depth in Chapter 11.

At a Glance ...

Basic obedience training is essential so your Bulldog puppy grows into a well-behaved and reliable adult. The basic cues of *sit, stay, down, come,* and *heel,* as well as *take it* and *leave it* will not only teach your puppy good manners but also can save your dog's life.

. . . .

It's best to solve problem behaviors while your Bulldog is a puppy before they become bad habits that are hard to break. Chewing, barking, and jumping up are three of the most common household problems, and they are all natural, instinctive canine behaviors. Get to the root of the problem and find out why your Bulldog is doing something he shouldn't; only then can you address and solve the problem effectively.

. . . .

No dog is perfect. If you have trouble training your dog, seek out a professional trainer. Ask your local breed club for recommendations or consult organizations such as the Association of Pet Dog Trainers (www.apdt.com) or the Certification Council for Professional Dog Trainers (www.ccpdt .org) to find the right trainer for you and your dog.

. . . .

Ready for more advanced training? Sign up for the AKC Canine Good Citizen® Program with a local trainer. Your Bulldog will learn advanced obedience training that will allow him to better socialize with the world and people around him. Learn more at www.akc.org/events.cgc.

CHAPTER EIGHT

Eat Up, Bulldog!

Few dog owner decisions are more confusing—or more critical—than the selection of food. A high-quality diet appropriate for your Bulldog's age and lifestyle will provide the proper balance of protein, carbohydrates, vitamins, minerals, and fatty acids necessary to support healthy bones, muscles, skin, and coat. Major dog-food manufacturers have developed formulas with strict quality controls, using fresh, natural ingredients from reliable sources.

Most new owners opt to feed their Bulldog puppies the same food the breeder had been offering.

In the world of dog food, there are enough choices to befuddle even experienced dog folks. Don't be intimidated by all those dog-food bags and cans on the store shelves. Read each label (how else can you learn what's in the food?) and check the food manufacturer's website if you want to learn more. Ask your breeder and your vet what food they recommend for your Bulldog. A basic knowledge of canine nutrition will provide the tools you need to offer your dog a diet that is best for his long-term health.

BALANCED DIETS

Store-bought dog foods can claim they are "complete and balanced" only if they meet the standards set forth by the Association of American Feed Control Officials (AAFCO). The food labels tell you what products are in the food (beef, chicken, corn, etc.), and list the ingredients in descending order of weight or amount. Do your research and purchase a high-quality diet for your Bulldog. Here's a short explanation of the types of nutrients you'll see on a dog-food label:

• **Carbohydrates:** Broken down and converted into sugars, carbohydrates are the main energy source for your dog's body.

• **Fats:** Fats act as a backup, stored energy source when carbohydrates are lacking. Fats are also essential for the production of hormones and nervous-system function.

• **Proteins:** Proteins are important for immune-system function as well as reparation of muscles, bones, and body tissues.

• **Vitamins and minerals:** Vitamins and minerals play a vital role in growth, healing, and muscular and nervous function.

• **Water:** All dogs must stay hydrated in order to wash away toxins and waste in their bodies, keeping their body systems functioning properly. Always provide access to ample water at all times to keep your Bulldog healthy.

Essential nutrients in correct proportions are the cornerstone of a healthy diet, so research what's available and shop around. Although dogs are carnivores, Bulldogs cannot tolerate foods that are extremely high in protein. Too much meat or protein-high kibble can cause itchy skin irritations known as "hot spots." Too much protein has also been known to cause kidney problems in Bulldogs.

DRY, WET, OR SEMI-MOIST?

Walking through the pet-supply store, you'll notice different types of dog food. Dry, wet, and semi-moist are the most popular foods on the market, and you'll have to do some research to decide which is best for your Bulldog based on his lifestyle and eating habits. Dry food is often the most economical, allowing you to purchase food in bulk. However, if your dog is underweight or dehydrated, wet canned food may be a better option. Semi-moist is one of the most expensive options, but most dogs find it the tastiest—a popular choice for finicky eaters. Consult with your veterinarian on which type of food to feed your Bulldog.

• **Kibble:** Dry food, or kibble, is a healthy, less expensive choice. It has some definite advantages over other types of dog food. Because it is cut into bite-size pieces and baked in bulk, it does not spoil quickly. It also helps clean your dog's teeth as he crunches down on the kibble, scraping plaque and tartar from his teeth and gums. If you are worried about the dull taste of dry food, fear not. It is tested and researched by a variety of scientists and veterinary nutritionists to be appealing to your dog and healthy for him according to U.S. Food and Drug Administration and AAFCO standards. If you still want to add a little variety to your Bulldog's dry food diet, try mixing a little canned food or semi-moist food with the kibble every now and then. Adding water or low-salt broth will help soften dry food for aging Bulldogs with sensitive teeth and gums.

• **Semi-moist:** Semi-moist food is an attractive choice for picky eaters. It is soft to the bite and is cut into shapes that resemble treats, making it easier for elderly dogs to chew and more appetizing for finicky eaters. Like kibble, semi-moist food is tested and formulated with nutrition in mind, however it is often

The Truth about Table Scraps

It's a rare dog owner who can resist the hopeful and pleading eyes of a Bulldog at the dinner table and not quickly slip a tiny piece of steak (minus the A1 Sauce) to the dog. But offering table scraps encourages begging behavior, and you may inadvertently make your dog sick. There are certain foods we enjoy that cannot be processed by the canine digestive system. It's safer to just feed your Bulldog food made specially for dogs.

A PIECE OF HISTORY

Winston Churchill was called the "British Bulldog," having fought for the rights and safety of British citizens during World War II and throughout his two terms as Prime Minister in the 1940s and 1950s. To this day, Winston is one of the most popular Bulldog names in both the United States and the United Kingdom.

Stay Lean

Lean is healthy; fat is not. Research has proven that obesity is a major canine killer. Quite simply, a lean dog lives longer than one that is overweight. And a lean dog that can run, jump, and play without the burden of those extra pounds has a much better quality of life. If your Bulldog needs to lose some weight, formulate a healthy eating and exercise plan for him under the guidance of your vet. Reducing calories does not mean reducing nutrition.

made with chemicals and artificial coloring to make it more appealing to owners and dogs. Check the label, and look for nutritional value before feeding it to your Bulldog. High amounts of corn syrup or artificial sweeteners can cause your dog to gain weight, and it will take a toll on his dental health.

• **Canned:** Canned food incorporates meat and meat by-products in delicious gravy. It contains mostly water—up to 70 percent by weight in some brands—which keeps your dog hydrated better than kibble or semi-moist foods. Canned food has a long shelf life, and it is prepackaged in perfect proportions for your pup. The down side of canned food is its cost. All leftovers must be refrigerated, and once a can is opened, it will spoil quickly. Also, its high water content can cause diarrhea in some dogs as well as plaque and tartar buildup on teeth.

LIFESTAGE FORMULAS

Many dog-food brands offer diets for every size, age, and activity level. As with human infants, puppies require a diet different than adults. Senior Bulldogs also require a different formula because their metabolism begins to slow as they age. Choose your dog food carefully based on your dog's age, weight, and lifestyle. Every dog is different and may require a slightly different formula of food.

Feeding a Puppy

If you're bringing home a Bulldog puppy, continue feeding him the same diet his breeder gave him. High-quality breeders usually feed their dogs high-quality food. Abrupt diet changes can cause stomach upset, especially in a puppy's immature physiology. The stress of leaving his mother and littermates may be enough to send your Bulldog's digestive tract into a tailspin; there's no sense adding to it. Moreover, diarrhea can be very dangerous for a puppy. Rapid dehydration can cause serious health problems or even death.

If for some reason you cannot continue feeding your puppy the same food as the breeder, make the change to a different diet gradually by adding a few teaspoons of the new food to his old food. Slowly increase the amount of new food in the mix, decreasing the old food amount proportionally. If your Bulldog likes the taste of the new food and isn't experiencing any physical problems, continue incorporating it until the changeover is complete.

Young puppies should be fed three or four small meals a day. Their little stomachs cannot handle larger amounts of food in one sitting. As your puppy grows, you can gradually reduce the frequency of his meals until he's eating twice a day by his first birthday—once in the morning and again in the evening. Puppies and young adults expend a great deal of energy, and their bodies need a frequent, regular energy source. The constant supply of nutrition will give your growing Bulldog the stamina he needs. Twice-daily feedings will also help regulate his elimination habits. Although your pup probably has the hang of going potty outside by the time he is one year old, his bladder and bowels are still developing. A meal will jump-start the need for elimination. Take him outside after mealtime and praise him when he goes. This is one of the few potty times you can predict!

Feeding an Adult

A Bulldog is considered an adult when he finishes growing, around twelve to eighteen months of age. A high-quality adult food will have all the nutrients he needs. There are even dog-food formulas for less active adults, in case your Bulldog doesn't get enough exercise. It's more likely that a Bulldog just crossing over from puppyhood to adulthood will still have loads of energy, and he'll need solid nutrition to keep him healthy and hearty.

An adult Bulldog should be fed twice a day, taking care not to overfeed him at each sitting. Gobbling food and overeating can lead to gastric torsion, or bloat, a life-threatening condition which can cause a painful death. Barrel-chested breeds like the Bulldog seem especially prone to the condition, so monitor how much, how fast, and how often your Bulldog eats.

Foods to Avoid

The best food for your Bulldog is dog food, not people food. Keep in mind that certain foods are toxic to dogs and can harm their health, causing problems such as anemia, paralysis, even death. No matter how convincing your Bulldog's plea, never give him any of the following:

- Alcohol
- Chocolate
- Coffee or tea
- Grapes or raisins
- Nuts
- Nicotine/tobacco
- Onions
- Broccoli
- Artificial sweeteners

Free-Feeding Frenzy

Some people may tell you that free-feeding is fine for your Bulldog; however, it often leads to excessive weight gain or weight loss or will make your dog finicky about his food. It is better to get your Bulldog on a regular feeding schedule.

Feeding a Senior

The age at which Bulldogs are considered senior citizens varies from dog to dog. Some may show signs of aging at six, while others are still going strong at eight. Even the eternally young-at-heart Bulldog will sleep more, tire more easily, and move more slowly, necessitating a decrease in caloric intake. As a dog ages, his metabolism slows down, and the pounds can add up. A senior Bulldog's organs will also function less efficiently, and his digestive system can become more sensitive to upsets. A change in diet, including smaller food portions, usually does the trick.

Your Bulldog may become finicky as he ages and turn up his already turned-up nose at food he's enjoyed for years. If that happens, try pouring a little vegetable broth over his kibble, or adding a tablespoon of cottage cheese to his wet or semi-moist food. Be aware that finicky eating is one thing, but loss of appetite is another. If your Bulldog shows no interest in eating, consult your veterinarian right away.

ALTERNATIVE DIETS

Although commercially produced dog foods are the most popular, there are other options. If your dog is an especially picky eater, or if he is sensitive to certain ingredients in his diet, you may want to consult your veterinarian or veterinary nutritionist regarding some alternative diets for your Bulldog. Many owners like knowing exactly what is going through their dogs' digestive systems, and raw food or home-cooked diets do just that.

The Raw Food Diet

Some dog owners are returning to their dogs' evolutionary roots by feeding them the Biologically Appropriate Raw Food (BARF) diet. The BARF diet is not as simple as tossing your Bulldog an uncooked hamburger patty. Nutritional requirements are just as important—if not more so—and warrant ample research.

The first thought that may come to mind is, "Won't my dog get sick from eating raw meat?" The answer is no, provided that the meat is of good quality and

handled properly. A dog's digestive system contains probiotic bacteria to digest meat and prevent illness. Human digestive systems have long evolved from this internal tolerance, which is why we can get sick from undercooked meat. For a dog, however, the fresher the food, the greater the nutrient availability.

Proponents of the BARF diet claim that the food, which is free of preservatives and other additives, strengthens their dogs' immune systems, and that their dogs have shinier coats and fewer skin problems, cleaner teeth, fresher breath, and vitality to spare. Some pet stores sell commercial raw food for dogs found in the refrigerated section. This food is individually packaged to make feeding safe and simple. Check with your veterinarian and do your homework on the pros and cons of a raw food diet.

The Home-Cooked Diet

This diet falls in between commercial and raw food diets. Some dog owners are picky about the food their Bulldogs eat and are not content to open a can or tear into a bag. They want the reassurance of knowing that the meals they serve their dogs are good enough for humans.

Home-cooked diets also require plant matter and nutrients found in bones, so they must be supplemented. It's best to consult with your veterinarian or veterinary nutritionist before starting your Bulldog on a home-cooked-only diet.

TREATS

Treats are indispensable training tools, but it's important to know what's inside your Bulldog's favorite treats. Commercial dog treats come in all shapes and sizes, and some are healthy and wholesome, while others contain mostly chemicals and animal by-products. The least expensive treats may not be the healthiest choice, as they tend to have little nutritional value. These treats are like junk food—instead, opt for healthier, more natural treats.

Some of the tastiest and handiest dog treats are right in your kitchen. Offer your Bulldog a slice of apple, a strip of bell pepper, or a tiny cube of cheese. Rice cakes and Cheerios are also satisfying snacks. And the blob of peanut butter in which you bury your dog's medication is a delicacy your dog can enjoy all by itself. Remember to check with your vet before experimenting with treat-worthy foods from your kitchen.

THE BOTTOM LINE

What you feed your Bulldog is a major factor in his overall health and longevity. It's worth your time and money to provide the best diet for your dog. With advice from your vet and ample research, you can find a nutritious diet for your Bulldog that is appropriate for his age, size, and activity level.

At a Glance ...

Know how to interpret dog-food labels, and take your breeder's and vet's advice regarding the best diet for your Bulldog's life stage and activity level.

. . . .

Puppies need more frequent feedings in smaller amounts. The schedule changes as the dog grows, usually to twice a day, once in the morning and once in the evening.

. . . .

Clean, cool water must be available to your Bulldog at all times. In warm weather, dogs will drink more often, so it's especially important that brachycephalic (short-muzzled) breeds like the Bulldog have access to water all day.

. . . .

Keep a close eye on your Bulldog's weight to be sure that he is neither under nor overweight, and consult a veterinarian if you want to alter your Bulldog's diet to supplement or reduce his weight.

CHAPTER NINE

A Wrinkled Beauty

Grooming is about more than primping. The one-on-one contact gives you a chance to bond with your Bulldog, and it's a good time to check his coat, face, and skin for any cuts, scrapes, or unusual bumps. A once-over for external parasites is also a good idea, even if your Bulldog is treated regularly with a parasite preventive.

When it comes to coat care, your Bulldog is a wash-and-wear breed that requires simple,

Check your Bulldog's eyes and ears daily for any irritation or redness. If there is any dirt or discharge, ask your vet to take a closer look.

regular brushing. His ears, teeth, and nails also need regular grooming. However, your Bulldog's facial wrinkles do call for special attention.

COAT

The short coat of a Bulldog doesn't warrant the extensive maintenance of a Poodle or Pomeranian. The Bulldog's fur itself is short, flat, and naturally glossy, so "hair care" is minimal—regular brushing is all that is required. Brushing distributes the natural oils that keep his coat shiny and his skin lubricated. It also helps prevent dandruff and eliminates any surface dirt in the coat. Brushing your Bulldog with a soft-bristled rubber brush a few times a week will keep your dog's coat looking shiny and clean. Most Bulldogs enjoy being brushed and relish the one-on-one time with their owners.

During your Bulldog's shedding times, which occur in the spring and fall, daily brushing will help keep shed hair around the home to a minimum, as the dead hair is caught in the brush, not left on your carpets and furniture. A grooming mitt that fits over your hand works well on the close coat of the Bulldog.

BATH TIME!

The Bulldog's short coat means he won't need a bath as often as some of his longer-haired cousins. In fact, too frequent bathing can dry out his skin and cause itching or a rash. Frequency of bathing will depend on your Bulldog's lifestyle. If he is a therapy dog that visits hospitals and nursing homes, he may need a bath prior to every visit, as required by the organization or facility. If he loves digging in the dirt and frolicking in the mud, he will need a bath more often than a Bulldog that prefers lounging on the couch. In warm weather, you can make bath time a fun game outdoors.

You can bathe your Bulldog in your bathtub, in a sink, or outdoors in warm weather. Wherever you choose, make sure you have a faucet or hose within reach to thoroughly soak and rinse his coat. When bathing your dog, remember to use a dog shampoo specially formulated for his sensitive skin. Human shampoos contain too much harsh detergent that can dry out your Bulldog's skin. Be careful

not to get shampoo in his eyes or ears. Place a small cotton ball in each ear to prevent water from getting in during a bath. After the bath, clean your dog's ears with a special solution or with mineral oil.

Mineral oil is also a lifesaver if you accidentally get soap in your Bulldog's eyes. Use your hand as a shield to prevent soapy water from running into your dog's eyes, but in case it does, rinse the eyes with clear, warm water. Apply a drop of mineral oil in the corner of each eye to soothe the irritation. Gently massage the skin over the eyeball to distribute the oil.

If you're bathing your Bulldog indoors, make sure the room temperature is warm enough so he doesn't get a chill. Lay a rubber mat on the bottom of the tub or sink so he doesn't lose his footing. You want bath time to be enjoyable, not stressful. And don't forget to wear clothes you don't mind getting wet!

Lift your Bulldog gently into the tub, making sure his footing is secure before you release him. Wet down his entire coat with warm water from a spray nozzle or shower hose, taking care not to spray his face directly. Thoroughly wet his coat, apply shampoo down his back (not on the head and face) and work it into a lather, getting all of the hard-to-reach places. For the face, use a lathered-up washcloth, making sure to clean all of the wrinkles. Wipe down both sides of the ear flaps with the washcloth.

Did You Know?

The Bulldog comes in a variety of colors and patterns including brindle, red, white, fawn, and piebald. Black Bulldogs are also common, and though undesirable as show dogs, they still make great pets.

When dogs play outdoors, they sometimes get stuff in their ears, such as seeds, burrs, and foxtails—anything that tends to stick to fur. Check your Bulldog's ears for these things when he comes in from playing outside. If left in the ear, they will cause your dog pain and possibly even damage his hearing. If you find something and cannot safely remove it at home, take your dog to the vet right away.

Now it's time to rinse. It's important that you don't skimp on this step; soap residue can leave your dog's coat dull and his skin itchy and flaky. Continue to rinse the coat, including the legs and underbelly, until the water runs clear. When you're sure no soap remains on his coat, carefully lift him out of the tub onto a floor or bath mat, again making sure he has his balance before you let go. Once you release him, he'll shake the excess water out of his coat, which is why you should wear clothes you don't mind getting wet! Use heavy towels to dry him as best as you can. Pay special attention to his paws and between his toes. Make sure all those nooks and crannies created by his wrinkles are thoroughly dry.

You should keep him indoors and away from drafts until he is completely dry. Some breeders recommend a bit of petroleum jelly on the Bulldog's nose following a bath to help keep it soft. If you need to dry your Bulldog quickly, a blow-dryer on the lowest heat, held at a safe distance, will do the trick.

WRINKLE CARE

Those wrinkles, the extra folds of skin that are part and parcel of the Bulldog's distinctive look, require special attention. One of the reasons Bulldogs are not for everyone is the extra commitment required for regular skin care. The face folds, in particular, need frequent cleaning. Dirt and bacteria can collect inside the wrinkles where air or towels don't reach easily. Dirty wrinkles not only smell bad but also can lead to skin discomfort and infection. Some dogs require a full wrinkle cleaning only once or twice a week, while others need it daily. Once you determine your Bulldog's wrinkle-care needs, be religious about it. Ongoing wrinkle care will keep your Bulldog smelling sweet and feeling comfortable.

Dog Grooming Shopping List

Here are the items you need to groom your Bulldog:

BATHING
- [ ] A handheld spray attachment for your tub or sink
- [ ] A rubber mat for the dog to stand on
- [ ] A tearless dog shampoo and conditioner (don't use human products)
- [ ] Towels (a chamois is best)
- [ ] A pet hair dryer (you can use your own, but set it on low)
- [ ] Spritz-on dry shampoo (handy in case you need a quick cleanup to get rid of dirt or odor)
- [ ] Mineral oil (in case you get water in the eyes)

BRUSHING COAT
- [ ] Short-bristled brush
- [ ] Metal comb and grooming mitt

WRINKLE CARE
- [ ] Small, soft cloth
- [ ] Baby wipes and cotton balls
- [ ] Petroleum jelly
- [ ] Antiseptic ointment or diaper-rash cream
- [ ] Powder or cornstarch (as a drying agent)

TRIMMING NAILS
- [ ] Dog nail cutters (scissor- or guillotine-type)
- [ ] Nail file or grinder
- [ ] Styptic powder or cornstarch (in case you cut the quick)

BRUSHING TEETH
- [ ] Dog toothbrush or child's toothbrush
- [ ] Dog toothpaste (don't use human toothpaste)

CLEANING EARS
- [ ] Cotton balls or wipes
- [ ] Liquid ear-cleaning solution or mineral oil

WIPING EYES
- [ ] Dog eye wipes or hydrogen peroxide
- [ ] Cotton balls

All you need to tend to your Bulldog's wrinkles is a damp cloth or cotton balls. Baby wipes are also convenient as gentle wrinkle cleaners, especially if they contain aloe. With a washcloth or cotton balls, mix a tiny dab of dog shampoo in a cup of warm water. Dip the cotton balls or cloth into the solution and gently wipe inside your Bulldog's wrinkle folds. Even though you're using only a tiny amount of shampoo, wipe the wrinkles clean with water to remove all soap residue.

Next, thoroughly dry the cleansed wrinkles with a soft cloth. Any remaining moisture on the skin, combined with a lack of air circulation, makes a perfect breeding ground for yeast and bacteria. The very purpose of regular wrinkle care can backfire if you don't dry the skin thoroughly after cleaning. Some people favor drying agents like powder or cornstarch to absorb excess moisture, but they can irritate the skin inside the folds if they clump. If you wish, spread a little petroleum jelly inside your Bulldog's face wrinkles to act as a moisture barrier (the face wrinkles get wet from drinking water all day long!) and to soothe any irritation.

If you notice any wrinkles that appear red or irritated, smooth on some antiseptic ointment or diaper-rash cream. If the soreness isn't healed within a week or so, consult your veterinarian.

EARS AND TEETH

Ear cleaning and tooth-brushing are also regular grooming tasks essential to your Bulldog's good health. Incorporate tooth-brushing as part of your Bulldog's face-washing routine. Purchase a dog toothbrush and dog toothpaste from your local pet-supply store. Some dog toothbrushes look like small versions of human toothbrushes, while others are made of soft rubber and are designed to slide over your index finger. Slowly accustom your pup to the feel of your finger in

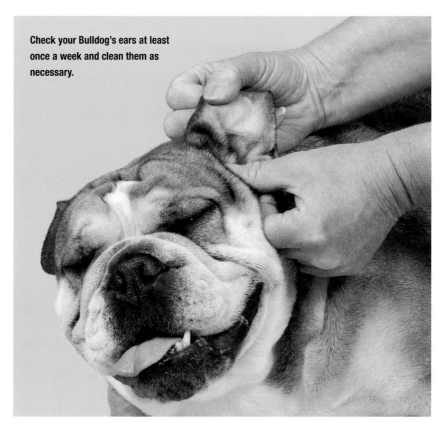

Check your Bulldog's ears at least once a week and clean them as necessary.

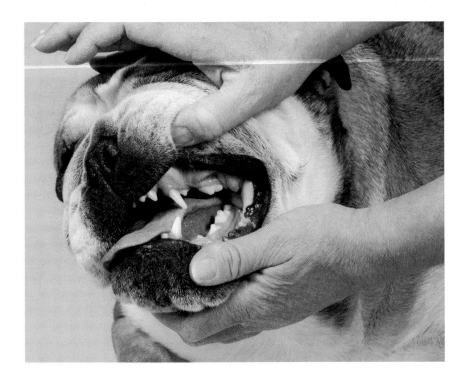

Good Teeth = Good Health

Home dental care is vital to your Bulldog's health. Studies prove that good oral hygiene can add three to five years to a dog's life. In other words, brushing your Bulldog's teeth means you'll have him around longer.

his mouth when he is young to get him used to the idea of brushing his teeth. Do this by sliding your finger over his teeth once or twice a day. Once he doesn't flinch, try using the toothbrush without paste. Again, once he is used to this, try putting a little dog toothpaste—never use people toothpaste as it can make him sick!—on the brush and move it in circular motions on the outside of his teeth. Be sure to massage his gums as well, but don't push too hard because you don't want to hurt your dog. You should brush your Bulldog's teeth at least two or three times a week.

Ears should be checked regularly and kept free of wax and debris. Using an ear-cleaning product and a soft cotton wipe, gently clean the inside of the ear, never probing deeper than you can see or into the ear canal. Any foul odor, thick discharge, or dark specks in the ear should be brought to your veterinarian's attention as this may be a sign of ear infection or ear mites.

NAIL-TRIMMING

Regular nail care is not indulgent; it's necessary. Nails that are allowed to grow too long can make walking difficult, as well as catch on objects and possibly injure your Bulldog. In the extreme, nails can grow so long that they curl under and puncture the toe pad. Many people are reluctant to trim their dog's nails for fear of cutting the quick, the blood vessel that extends toward the tip of the nail, and hurting the Bulldog. Ironically, if nails are left untrimmed, the quick extends farther toward the nail tip, and you can't avoid cutting into it. If you don't have confidence in your nail-trimming skills, have the vet's office or dog groomer show you how to do it right.

Most young dogs won't sit still to have their nails clipped, so it's important to accustom your Bulldog to routine pedicures while he's still a puppy. That way he learns early on that the procedure is nothing to fear, and that cooperation will earn him an extra treat.

The first step is getting your puppy used to having his paws handled. Gently hold and stroke his feet when you're interacting with him. Praise him when he allows the handling and give him a treat to reinforce the positive behavior.

Next, familiarize him with the nail clippers before you actually use them on him. Now it's time to trim your Bulldog's nails. Quickly snip the tip of each nail on one foot. Praise and reward your puppy before moving on to the next foot. If he wants to frolic a little at the sound of your verbal praise, let him do so before moving on to the next set of nails. This gives him a chance to release any anxiety or tension he may associate with the nail-trimming procedure. Repeat the pattern of cut, praise, reward, and play until all four paws are done. Your Bulldog will soon learn that it's worth having someone handle his feet if it results in treats and loving attention!

While you will do your best to avoid cutting the quick, accidents will sometimes happen. If you cut the quick, stop the bleeding with styptic powder or cornstarch. Later on, try to go back to trimming his nails and see how your Bulldog reacts. If he is fearful, start the acclimation process all over again until he's forgotten the incident and has only the rewards on his mind.

How do you know exactly where the quick is? If your dog's nails are white, the quick is clearly visible—it's the pink vein that runs through the middle of the nail—and easily avoided. If your Bulldog's nails are black, the quick is harder to see, so err on the side of caution and clip just a little of his nail at a time. Alternatively, you can use a file or motorized grinding tool to sand down your Bulldog's nails. You can also use the file or grinder to smooth the rough edges left behind after nail-trimming that can catch on fabric or scratch your skin.

If you opt to trim your dog's nails using a grinder or file, you need to introduce the noise and vibration of the tool to your dog before you actually begin the procedure. Turn on the grinder while you're doing something else with your Bulldog, such as cleaning his wrinkles or brushing his coat, so he gets used to the noise of the motor. If he seems unfazed, touch the grinder's handle to one of his paws so he can feel the vibration. If the noise and vibration don't bother him, try grinding a nail. If he's okay with that, do an entire set, and then take a play break. Soon your Bulldog will have a pedicure a Poodle would envy.

WRAP IT UP

A Bulldog is easy to groom once you get into a routine. Brush him regularly, trim his toenails every week or so, and wipe him down with a damp cloth in between baths. Watch the folds around his face, eyes, and muzzle, and clean them on a daily basis, if necessary. Give him a bath as needed. With these grooming skills, you will have a good-looking, fresh-smelling Bulldog with whom you will be proud to be seen!

A clean Bulldog is a healthy Bulldog. Bathe your dog once a month and thoroughly clean his eyes, ears, and wrinkles regularly.

At a Glance ...

Your Bulldog's short coat makes his coat-care needs minimal; regular brushing will remove debris and dead hair from his coat. Incorporate your "housekeeping" tasks into the grooming routine—tooth-brushing, eye care, ear care, and nail-trimming.

. . . .

Bathing too frequently will dry out your Bulldog's skin and coat; a bath once a month is enough unless your dog gets into something really dirty.

. . . .

Check your Bulldog's wrinkles every day and clean them as often as necessary.

CHAPTER TEN

The Healthy Bulldog

Keeping your Bulldog in the peak of health requires care, commitment, and a good partnership with your veterinarian. Exercise, good nutrition, vaccinations, and annual checkups are just a few of the things a responsible owner does to keep his Bulldog healthy and thriving.

During your Bulldog's weekly grooming sessions, take a thorough look at your dog's body. Feel his ribs and look at his ears, eyes,

mouth, teeth, and gums. Regularly observe him and watch how he moves. Is he limping? Is his gait different? Monitoring your Bulldog's day-to-day behavior will help you catch any health problems as early as possible. Your efforts to keep him healthy and hardy will be rewarded with more time with your Bulldog's bright eyes and happy, crooked smile.

THE BEST HEALTH CARE

Good Bulldog health care requires the same commonsense guidelines we use for ourselves: eat a balanced, nutritious diet; get regular exercise; and manage stress. Our pets depend totally on us for their existence, so we owe it to them to provide the best care possible.

VITAL VETERINARY CARE

Make sure your dog is seen by the veterinarian at least once a year. This includes a routine physical exam during which the vet will check your Bulldog's general health. He or she will listen to your dog's heart and lungs; palpate the abdomen, muscles, and joints; check the eyes and ears; and look inside the mouth for any tooth or gum problems. The vet will also check the dog's coat as an indicator of overall health. A clean, shiny coat is the hallmark of a healthy dog; a dull coat with dandruff may indicate an underlying health issue.

Be ready to answer your vet's questions about your Bulldog's daily diet, bathroom habits, and disposition. If you have any specific questions for the vet, make a list to bring with you to the appointment so you don't forget anything. It's also important for you to let your veterinarian know of any changes you have seen in your dog since his last well-dog checkup.

CORE Vaccines
Check with your vet, but all puppies should receive vaccines for the following diseases.

CONDITION	TREATMENT	PROGNOSIS	VACCINE NEEDED
ADENOVIRUS-2 (immunizes against Adenovirus-1, the agent of infectious canine hepatitis)	No curative therapy for infectious hepatitis; treatment geared toward minimizing neurologic effects, shock, hemorrhage, secondary infections	Self-limiting but cross-protects against infectious hepatitis, which is highly contagious and can be mild to rapidly fatal	Recommended
DISTEMPER	No specific treatment; supportive treatment (IV fluids, antibiotics)	High mortality rates	Highly recommended
PARVOVIRUS-2	No specific treatment; supportive treatment (IV fluids, antibiotics)	Highly contagious to young puppies; high mortality rates	Highly recommended
RABIES	No treatment	Fatal	Required

THE FIRST VISIT

Before you bring your puppy home, you need to find a qualified veterinarian with experience treating Bulldogs, who is knowledgeable about the potential problems and conditions commonly seen in the breed. Ask your breeder, dog-owning friends, or check with your local Bulldog club for vet referrals in your area.

Take your puppy to the vet within the first few days of bringing him home for an overall checkup. This will establish your Bulldog as a patient and give you and your dog the chance to get acquainted with the vet. On your first visit, take along the puppy's health records that you received from the breeder. These papers will have a record of the vaccinations your puppy has received so the veterinarian will know how to continue your Bulldog's vaccination schedule. You should also take in a fecal sample for a worm test. Try to make the visit as pleasant as possible for

If possible, stop by the veterinarian's office on your way home from the breeder. Your new puppy can meet the office staff, and when you return in a couple of days for his exam, your Bulldog won't be as anxious.

A PIECE OF HISTORY

The Bulldog Club of America (BCA) was first established in 1890 by a group of Bulldog owners in the northeastern United States. The group was one of the first breed clubs to be recognized by the American Kennel Club. The BCA was reorganized in 1950 to accommodate the rise in membership and popularity of the breed. Today, the Bulldog is ranked sixth in the nation in AKC registrations.

Preventing Heatstroke

Heatstroke should be regarded as the life-threatening condition it is, and care should always be taken to prevent it, especially with Bulldogs and other brachycephalic breeds. Never leave your Bulldog in a parked car or unsupervised outdoors in the yard. He can overheat more quickly than you may think and pay the price with his life.

To protect your Bulldog from heatstroke:

• DON'T leave him in a parked car, even if you think it's pleasant outside and the car windows are down.

• DON'T take him jogging with you.

• DON'T leave him unsupervised anywhere outside.

• DON'T let him play to the point of overheating, even indoors.

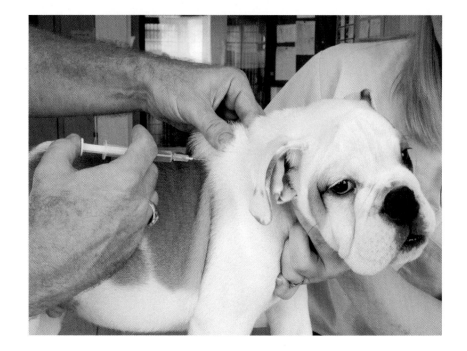

your pup, so he will regard future vet visits as fun excursions. Your Bulldog will look to you for cues about what's happening, so keep your mood light. If you are comfortable with your vet, your Bulldog will be, too.

Try to find a veterinarian who is within 10 miles of your home, not just for convenience, but also in case of an emergency. Find a veterinarian you feel comfortable talking to—after all, he or she will be a trusted resource for many years. Make sure the office looks and smells clean. Ask about fees for services before setting up an appointment. Many veterinary clinics have several vets practicing there, so ask to see the same vet for each visit, as he or she will personally know the history of your dog, and your dog will become familiar with the individual. Inquire if the clinic takes emergency calls and, if they do not, get the name, address, and telephone number of the nearest emergency veterinary clinic or hospital to keep on file.

Your Bulldog puppy will visit the vet every few weeks for his vaccinations. As an adult, your Bulldog will need booster shots, the frequency of which will vary. Regardless of vaccine frequency, an adult Bulldog should visit the veterinarian once a year for a full checkup, including an annual heartworm test and dental cleaning. Most importantly, the annual visit keeps your vet apprised of your pet's health progress, and the hands-on exam may turn up problems and small abnormalities that you may not see or feel. As your dog reaches his senior years, around the age of seven, he should see the vet twice yearly, as the health care for senior dogs is more extensive. Plus, more frequent visits allow the vet to catch any health problems as early as possible, which can make a big difference in the success of the treatment and cure.

VACCINATIONS

One of the first things your vet will do is set up a schedule for your pup's vaccinations. Vaccine protocol for puppies varies among veterinarians, but most recommend a series of three "combination" shots given at three- to four-week intervals.

Your puppy should have had his first shot before he left his breeder. Combination shots vary, and a single injection may contain five, six, seven, or even eight vaccines. Many breeders and veterinarians feel the potency in high-combination vaccines can negatively compromise a puppy's immature immune system, so they recommend fewer vaccines per shot or even separating vaccines into individual injections. That means additional visits to your veterinarian, but your Bulldog's healthy immune system is worth it. Talk with your vet about the pros and cons of different vaccination schedules to decide what is best for your Bulldog.

The vaccines recommended by the American Veterinary Medical Association (AVMA) are called "core" vaccines, those which protect against diseases most dangerous to your puppy and adult dog. These include distemper, canine parvovirus, canine adenovirus, and canine hepatitis. These core vaccinations are generally combined into one injection. Rabies immunization is required by law in all fifty states, and the vaccine is usually given at least three weeks after the complete series of puppy shots.

Other Vaccines and Treatment

Depending on where you live and your dog's needs, the following ailments and diseases can be treated through your veterinarian.

CONDITION	TREATMENT	PROGNOSIS	RECOMMENDATION
BORDETELLA (KENNEL COUGH)	Keep warm; humidify room; moderate exercise	Highly contagious; rarely fatal in healthy dogs; easily treated	Optional; prevalence varies; vaccine may be linked to acute reactions; low efficacy
FLEA AND TICK	Topical and ingestible	Highly contagious	Highly recommended
HEARTWORM	Arsenical compound; rest; restricted exercise	Widely occurring infections; preventive programs available regionally; successful treatment after early detection	Preventive treatment highly recommended
INTESTINAL WORMS	Dewormer; home medication regimen	Good with prompt treatment	Highly recommended
LYME DISEASE	Antibiotics	Can't completely eliminate the organism, but can be controlled in most cases	Recommended only for dogs with high risk of exposure to deer ticks
PARAINFLUENZA	Rest; humidify room; moderate exercise	Highly contagious; mild; self-limiting; rarely fatal	Optional but recommended; doesn't block infection, but lessens clinical signs
PERIODONTITIS	Dental cleaning; extractions; repair	Excellent, but involves anesthesia	Recommended

"Non-core" vaccines are optional and are usually dependent on where you live and on your Bulldog's lifestyle—these factors will determine which diseases, if any, your Bulldog is at risk for. The most common non-core vaccines are for canine parainfluenza, leptospirosis, canine coronavirus, Bordetella (kennel cough), and Lyme disease (borreliosis). Your veterinarian will alert you if there is a risk of these non-fatal diseases in your town or neighborhood so you can immunize accordingly.

To learn more about core and non-core vaccines recommended for your area, visit the website of the American Animal Hospital Association (AAHA), which offers a downloadable report on vaccinations at www.aahanet.org/Library/CanineVaccine.aspx. The AVMA has a helpful section on frequently asked questions about pet vaccinations at www.avma.org/issues/vaccination.

All dogs love spending time outdoors, but pesky fleas, ticks, and mosquitoes can carry fatal diseases. Be safe and talk to your vet about which parasite preventives are best for your Bulldog.

WHAT TO LOOK OUT FOR

While all physical conditions or diseases can strike any dog, certain illnesses are more commonly seen in some breeds than in others. This is true of the Bulldog. It's best to arm yourself with information on conditions often seen in Bulldogs so you can recognize the symptoms if they do develop.

Breathing

The Bulldog is a brachycephalic breed like the French Bulldog, Boxer, Boston Terrier, and other breeds that have flat faces. Because of their facial structures and short muzzles, all of these breeds can have difficulty breathing during hot weather. Care must be taken not to let your dog become overheated. Do not take your dog out for a run on a hot day, and never leave him out in the yard when it's over 80 degrees Fahrenheit. If it's too hot for you, then it's too hot for your dog. Although exercise is important for a Bulldog to build stamina and prevent obesity, don't overdo it, particularly when it is hot or humid. Always have shade and fresh water available for him.

Because of the breed's flat face, some Bulldogs may be affected with elongated palates. Your veterinarian should advise you about this issue. An elongated palate can cause excessive snoring and noisy breathing. This condition makes heatstroke a greater threat. Tell your vet if your Bulldog shows signs of labored breathing, as an elongated palate can be corrected through surgery.

Skin

The many wrinkles and folds on a Bulldog are perfect breeding grounds for skin problems, which is why regular wrinkle care is important. Rashes and irritations are usually not big problems by themselves, but they can lead to secondary infections which, if not treated, can become serious. Most skin conditions fall under the term *dermatitis*, but the cause and potential for secondary infection will determine which treatment your veterinarian recommends.

Certain skin ailments, such as wrinkle dermatitis or muzzle pyoderma, can affect any dog but are especially problematic for a wrinkly breed like the Bulldog. Clean the folds on your Bulldog's face and body as often as needed as part of your grooming routine. If a problem develops, see your veterinarian for antibiotics to clear it up. Vigilant wrinkle care, observation, and skin inspection can help prevent these problems before they start.

Joints

A common affliction for Bulldogs is luxating patella, a condition in which the kneecap slips out of place. Depending on the severity, the kneecap may pop back into place on its own, or it must be manually manipulated back into place by a veterinarian. Left untreated, a dog with luxating patella can develop osteoarthritis in the joint. The most severe cases require surgery. Because of the Bulldog's respiratory make-up, surgery should always be the last resort because general anesthesia is riskier for the Bulldog than for other breeds.

Hip dysplasia is also a concern in Bulldogs, as it is in many medium-sized and large breeds. With this inherited disease, the head of the femur (thigh bone)

Say Cheese!

Your dog's teeth are also an important part of his health care. In addition to regular brushing, have your vet examine your Bulldog's teeth during his annual checkup. Your veterinarian will let you know if your pup needs his pearly whites cleaned. If neglected, your dog's teeth will develop a buildup of tartar along the gum line that will cause gingivitis and tooth decay.

Periodontal disease is a major contributor to kidney disease; there is even a risk of damage to the heart, liver, and kidneys through bacteria that can enter your dog's bloodstream through his mouth. So keep on brushing—and don't forget to visit the doggy dentist regularly!

fails to fit into the socket of the hip bone, and there is not enough muscle mass to hold the joint together. This can often be very painful for the dog, causing him to limp or move about with great difficulty.

CREEPY-CRAWLIES

Though a nuisance, fleas are easily treated now with topical medications—no more messy powders and smelly collars. Other types of parasites are not as common, such as heartworm and intestinal worms, but you must still keep a lookout for signs and symptoms of parasites and get your Bulldog checked because some of the diseases these pests carry or transmit can be deadly.

Support Canine Health Research

AMERICAN KENNEL CLUB™

The mission of the American Kennel Club Canine Health Foundation, Inc. (AKC CHF) is to advance the health of all dogs and their owners by funding sound scientific research and supporting the dissemination of health information to prevent, treat, and cure canine disease. The foundation makes grants to fund:

- Identifying the cause(s) of disease
- Earlier, more accurate diagnosis
- Developing screening tests for breeders
- Accurate, positive prognosis
- Effective, efficient treatment

The AKC CHF also supports educational programs that bring scientists together to discuss their work and develop new collaborations to further advance canine health.

The AKC created the foundation in 1995 to raise funds to support canine health research. Each year, the AKC CHF allocates $1.5 million to new health research projects.

How You Can Help: If you have an AKC-registered dog, submit his DNA sample (cheek swab or blood sample) to the Canine Health Information Center (CHIC) DNA databank (www.caninehealthinfo.org). Encourage regular health testing by breeders, get involved with your local dog club, and support the efforts to host health education programs. And, if possible, make a donation.

For information, contact the AKC Canine Health Foundation, P.O. Box 900061, Raleigh, NC 27675-9061 or check out the website at www.akcchf.org.

Fleas and Mites

Fleas have been "bugging" dogs for millennia, and it's likely that you will wage many flea battles during your Bulldog's lifetime. Ticks and ear mites are also common, especially if your dog spends a lot of time rooting around the backyard. Fortunately, there are many effective weapons to aid in your flea, tick, and mite wars.

If you notice your dog scratching profusely, check his coat for fleas and his ears for mites. If you see black specks of dirt scattered across your Bulldog's belly or in your Bulldog's ears, it is a sure sign of fleas or ear mites. Your veterinarian will advise you which of the current products will be safest and most effective for your Bulldog. You can get prescription medications from your vet or over-the-counter products and treatments at pet-supply stores.

Fleas and mites can be a nuisance, because you not only have to kill the adult fleas on your dog but you also need to combat the fleas and eggs that may be on your furniture and in your carpet. The most effective method of flea control is a two-step approach.

First, address the fleas on your Bulldog. Your veterinarian will most likely prescribe a medication or recommend a specific over-the-counter treatment. Most of these are in the form of liquid droplets that are squeezed onto your dog's back in between his shoulder blades once a month. The drops slowly spread through your dog's coat, killing the fleas and eggs on his body. Other flea medications come in pill form, which you give to your dog in his food each month.

Second, address the fleas and eggs in your home. Purchase a pet-safe insect growth regulator and insecticide to spray around your home. Be sure to cover all

Spaying or Neutering

Should you or shouldn't you? Statistics prove that female dogs spayed before their first heat cycle have a 90-percent less risk of developing several common female cancers and other serious health problems such as uterine infection or ovarian tumors.

Males neutered before their hormones kick in, usually before six months of age, have a greatly reduced chance of getting testicular and prostate cancer and other related tumors and infections. Additionally, males will be less likely to roam, become aggressive, or display other overt male behaviors that owners find difficult to handle.

Obesity is a major health problem for dogs, so make sure to feed your Bulldog a nutritious diet and keep him active with daily walks and lots of playtime. He'll love it!

high-traffic areas of your home, including your dog's bed, the couch, and all carpets and other furniture. After a few hours, vacuum the area completely and then throw away the vacuum bag or, if you have a bagless vacuum, thoroughly clean out the vacuum's compartment. Discuss all options with your veterinarian.

Ticks

Ticks are more common in certain areas of the country, and these pests can carry diseases such as Lyme disease (borreliosis) and Rocky Mountain spotted fever that can spread to humans. Check with your vet to find out if ticks are common in your area. If so, your dog may need a few extra vaccinations to protect him.

Heartworm and Other Internal Parasites

Heartworms are parasites that propagate inside your dog's heart and can be fatal if left untreated. Contracted through mosquito bites, heartworms are a risk everywhere in the country. All dogs—even indoor ones—should take a heartworm preventive, which can be given daily or monthly in pill form, or in a shot every six months. Pills come in tasty flavors so your Bulldog thinks he's getting a treat instead of medication. Heartworm preventives require a prescription, so discuss which option will work best for your Bulldog with your veterinarian.

Roundworms, tapeworms, hookworms, threadworms, and whipworms are other internal parasites that can cause a host of problems. Most worms are evident in a dog's stool, which is why your dog's fecal sample is tested every year by the vet. If your Bulldog has digestive trouble or problems going to the bathroom, talk to your vet about testing your dog for these different types of worms. Puppies are dewormed as a matter of course, and adults that have internal parasites are prescribed an appropriate dewormer. Most heartworm preventives protect dogs against other internal parasites, so keep up on your dog's preventive medications, and he should stay heartworm- and parasite-free!

STAY ACTIVE

Despite the Bulldog's reputation for being less active than many other dogs, the breed is not genetically predisposed to obesity. With a healthy diet and daily exercise, your Bulldog will stay active and fit throughout his lifetime.

If you think your Bulldog may be overweight, feel around his torso. You should be able to easily feel his ribs through a thin layer of skin and muscle. Your Bulldog should have a definite waistline, and his stomach should gently tuck up underneath his abdomen. If your dog is more barrel-shaped, and your fingers sink through a layer of fat before reaching your dog's ribs, it's time for a change. Talk with your veterinarian about "light" or "senior" food options for your dog and the different ways you can exercise with him. Gradual weight loss is healthy weight loss. It may take a few months to get your dog back to his peak weight and energy level. At a healthy weight and with an active life, your Bulldog will live longer, have less medical problems as he ages, and be more energetic and comfortable.

At a Glance ...

Find a veterinarian who is experienced treating Bulldogs, with whom you are comfortable, who offers the services you need, and who is conveniently located. Take your Bulldog to the vet once a year for a well-dog checkup. Once your Bulldog becomes a senior citizen, around age seven, he should see the vet twice yearly so that any problems can be detected as early as possible.

Discuss your dog's vaccinations with your vet so that you can agree on a safe course of inoculation for your Bulldog. Core vaccines are a must, but non-core vaccines vary from area to area. Your veterinarian will help you decide which vaccinations are necessary for your dog.

Learn more about your Bulldog and what medical conditions are common in the breed. For the most up-to-date health information, refer to the breed's parent club, the Bulldog Club of America, at www.thebca.org.

Watch for any abnormal behaviors from your Bulldog between annual veterinary visits. If you have any questions or worries, call your veterinarian.

CHAPTER ELEVEN

The Bulldog in Action

All dogs thrive on mental, physical, and social stimulation, and organized dog activities are great ways to meet all these needs. It's not healthy for your Bulldog to be a couch potato. Like all dogs, what he really wants is to be active, and more importantly, to spend time with you, his favorite human. With a little guidance and conditioning, you and your Bulldog can get involved in a variety of sports and volunteer work that are physically and

Bulldogs enjoy moderate exercise just as much as more athletic breeds. Take your Bulldog on a walk at least twice a day to keep him mentally and physically healthy.

mentally stimulating. The time spent training your dog and participating with him in these activities will strengthen your bond and keep you both fit and active.

LET'S GET PHYSICAL

Before dogs were domesticated, their daily food-finding excursions were all the exercise they needed. Now that dogs lead a life of leisure with humans, it's our responsibility to make sure that exercise is part of their daily routine. Exercise doesn't just keep dogs physically fit; it keeps their minds busy and happy. Bored,

Junior Showmanship

AMERICAN KENNEL CLUB™

Junior Showmanship classes at dog shows, open to children ages nine to eighteen years old, offer the opportunity for budding fanciers to develop their handling skills and learn about good sportsmanship, dogs, and dog shows.

The competitions include handling and performance events, similar to those offered for adults. Judges evaluate the children's handling methods, rather than the animals, although the dogs do need to be registered with the AKC.

If your child shows interest in Junior Showmanship, encourage it! Many junior handlers continue in their love of dogs to become professional handlers, veterinarians, breeders, and trainers. Learn more about Junior Showmanship at www.akc.org/kids_juniors.

lonely, or anxious dogs often become destructive. Because dogs are social, active animals, they need lively interaction with other animals (including humans). Playing with another dog or a human meets the Bulldog's physical and emotional needs, as does a good walk or two every day. Make sure that your Bulldog doesn't exert himself too much in hot weather, and give him frequent water breaks and rest periods during playtime.

There are plenty of organized activities for you and your Bulldog: conformation, obedience, and Rally. Think a Bulldog can't cut it in the agility ring? Think again! Many Bulldogs have done well in agility and other sports. While they may not be stiff competition, Bulldogs will get some exercise and have a great time doing it. Before engaging in any kind of regular exercise program or activity, though, take your Bulldog in for a preliminary checkup with your vet to make sure there are no underlying health issues to prevent your dog from participating.

CONFORMATION

Anyone who has watched a dog show on television can tell you that there's something compelling about seeing those fine canine athletes going through their paces. The oldest dog sport, conformation showcases how well a dog "conforms" to its breed's standard. Your dog must be at least six months old and be registered with the American Kennel Club to participate in dog shows and most other AKC events. Because the goal of conformation is to identify ideal representatives for breeding, your Bulldog must be unaltered (not spayed or neutered).

There are three types of conformation shows: All-breed shows, Specialty shows, and Group shows. All-breed shows include competitions for more than 170 breeds and varieties. The biggest shows are often televised, such as the Westminster Dog Show or the AKC/Eukanuba National Championship. Specialty shows are usually hosted by the individual breed clubs and highlight a specific breed. Group shows incorporate all of the breeds within a group, such as the Non-Sporting Group, to which the Bulldog belongs. Each type of conformation show has categories, or "classes," in which dogs compete. The winners of each class compete against each other for championship points and awards such as Best of Breed and Best in Show.

If you think you'd like to become involved in dog showing, be sure to look for a show-quality Bulldog when searching for a puppy. Start by contacting a reputable breeder with conformation experience. The breeder will help you select a puppy with show potential and will explain the necessary steps you must take to raise a champion. Once you find the perfect puppy, contact your local breed club and visit the AKC website, www.akc.org/events/conformation, for more information about training classes and ways to get involved in conformation.

OBEDIENCE

The first Bulldog obedience trial was held in Northern California in 1970 and had an entry of nine Bulldogs. Since then, Bulldogs have done well in obedience, and numerous Bulldogs have earned titles in the sport. If you and your dog enjoyed basic obedience training and would like to do more, consider obedience competition, or trials, which test a dog's ability to follow your cues as you lead

Did You Know?

Only two Bulldogs have taken the top award at the prestigious Westminster Kennel Club Dog Show since it began in 1877. Ch. Strathtay Prince Albert won Best in Show in 1913 and was the first non-Terrier to win. In 1955, Ch. Kippax Fearnaught took the prize and was deemed by the judge to be "the best Bulldog I've ever seen."

Join the Club

Interested in partici-
pating in some sort of
activity with your Bull-
dog but not sure which?
Consider joining a local
Bulldog club or the
national club, the Bull-
dog Club of America
(www.thebca.org).
Through these organiza-
tions, you can find other
owners, participate in
Bulldog gatherings, find
information on educa-
tional seminars, and ask
more experienced own-
ers for advice.

him through different training exercises throughout the course. There are three
levels of obedience competition—Novice, Open, and Utility—each requiring the
dog to perform specific obedience skills at the handler's cues. Points are awarded
based on the difficulty level of the exercise, how well the handler communicates
with the dog, and how well the dog performs the exercise. At the lower levels of
completion, vocal cues are allowed, but at the Utility level, only hand signals may
be given. Be aware, though, that higher-level trials involve jumping and running—not a Bulldog's strong suits. Don't push him beyond his safe capabilities.
Learn more about the AKC's obedience program and the various titles your dog
can earn at www.akc.org/events/obedience.

Junior Scholarships

The American Kennel Club shows its commitment to supporting young people in
their interest in purebred dogs by awarding
thousands of dollars in scholarships to those competing in
Junior Showmanship. The scholarships range from $1,000
to $5,000 and are based on a person's academic achieve-
ments and his or her history with purebred dogs. Learn
more at www.akc.org/kids_juniors.

RALLY

Rally is a relatively new dog sport based on obedience, but it is less structured. This is a great way to introduce your Bulldog to competitive obedience, in a more relaxed environment. In Rally, dogs and their handlers negotiate a course containing ten to fifteen stations, some of which are jumps at the more advanced levels. At each station, directional signs are changed for each dog/handler team to keep the course exciting and unique. Both verbal cues and hand signals are permitted, but you cannot touch your dog. Rally, like obedience, can be a high-energy sport requiring a significant amount of running, jumping, and physical dexterity. Be sure to start training your Bulldog slowly, conditioning his body for this fun sport. Find out more about AKC Rally competitions at www.akc.org/events/rally.

Service Dogs

Service dog is the generic name for dogs trained to assist a physically or emotionally challenged person. A service dog must be able to endure inclement weather, distance walking, and have the ability to perform simple tasks. The Bulldog's physiology is not designed for this kind of work on a regular basis, making him a less-than-ideal choice for a career as a service dog. Of course, there are exceptions to every rule. Even if the Bulldog breed doesn't fill the bill as a Seeing Eye or hearing dog, there are a few service specialties that Bulldogs can perform quite well. So don't be surprised if you see a Bulldog wearing an "I'm working—please do not pet me" harness. You'll know right away that his human is in good paws.

• Psychiatric Service Dog: These dogs can be life-changing for people with mental disabilities. For example, someone with agoraphobia, the fear of open spaces, may be able to venture out in public with a Bulldog specially trained never to leave the handler's side. An autistic person can benefit from a service Bulldog trained to alert him or her to repetitive movements associated with autism.

• Seizure Alert/Response Dog: This dog is trained to respond to certain cues that a seizure is about to strike his human, and to either stay with the person or go get help. Some dogs are trained to touch a speed-dial button on the phone that dials 911 and to start barking when he hears a voice at the other end of the receiver.

The AKC Code of Sportsmanship

- Sportsmen respect the history, traditions, and integrity of the sport of purebred dogs.
- Sportsmen commit themselves to values of fair play, honesty, courtesy, and vigorous competition, as well as winning and losing with grace.
- Sportsmen refuse to compromise their commitment and obligation to the sport of purebred dogs by injecting personal advantage or consideration into their decisions or behavior.
- The sportsman judge judges only on the merits of the dogs and considers no other factors.
- The sportsman judge or exhibitor accepts constructive criticism.
- The sportsman exhibitor declines to enter or exhibit under a judge where it might reasonably appear that the judge's placements could be based on something other than the merits of the dogs.
- The sportsman exhibitor refuses to compromise the impartiality of a judge.
- The sportsman respects the American Kennel Club's bylaws, rules, regulations, and policies governing the sport of purebred dogs.
- Sportsmen find that vigorous competition and civility are not inconsistent and are able to appreciate the merit of their competition and the efforts of competitors.
- Sportsmen welcome, encourage, and support newcomers to the sport.
- Sportsmen will deal fairly with all those who trade with them.
- Sportsmen are willing to share honest and open appraisals of both the strengths and weaknesses of their breeding stock.
- Sportsmen spurn any opportunity to take personal advantage of positions offered or bestowed upon them.
- Sportsmen always consider as paramount the welfare of their dogs.
- Sportsmen refuse to embarrass the sport, the American Kennel Club, or themselves while taking part in the sport.

Tillman, the Bulldog spokesman for Natural Balance Pet Food, is a trained skateboarder, surfer, and snowboarder. Whether its an organized sport or just some backyard fun, Bulldogs excel at a variety of activities.

AGILITY

Bulldogs can compete in AKC agility. However, agility is a vigorous activity that requires speed and accuracy as the dog runs, jumps, and balances his way through an obstacle course that includes weave poles, tunnels, jumps, and other equipment. One of the challenges of agility is finding an adequate area to practice. The obstacles and equipment used in competition are large and can be expensive. Many local breed clubs offer practice courses nearby and conduct local practice matches. Seek out your local kennel club for more information.

If your Bulldog has any breathing problems, agility will be too strenuous for him—use good judgment when deciding whether or not to explore this particular sport with your Bulldog. If you do pursue agility, check with your veterinarian to discuss what physical conditioning your Bulldog will need, and what activities or events to avoid, if any. Be mindful of overheating, and go have a ball! To learn more about agility, visit www.akc.org/events/agility.

THERAPY

For a less athletic but equally, if not more so, rewarding pursuit, consider therapy work with your Bulldog. A good therapy dog displays sound temperament and is not startled or unnerved by strangers or new places. He must be patient, confident, and at ease in a variety of circumstances, from busy hospital wards to sedate retirement homes. Therapy dogs thrive on human contact because one of their main purposes is to allow both adults and children to pet and dote on them.

Because of the Bulldog's intelligence and friendly nature, therapy work may be the perfect activity for him.

If your Bulldog has these characteristics, he has the potential to become a therapy dog.

There are various organizations that train and certify dogs and their owners for pet therapy work, which consists of taking your dog to places like hospitals, nursing homes, schools, and care centers to visit the residents there, bringing companionship, comfort, and cuddles. If this sounds like something you are interested in, research the following programs and organizations to get started:

• **AKC's Canine Good Citizen® Program:** This is a two-part program that trains dogs to become well-mannered good canine citizens both at home and in the community. It requires dogs to train for and pass a ten-step test that proves a dog is ready to become involved in activities such as therapy work and obedience. Some of the steps include letting a friendly stranger approach and pet him, moving through a crowd calmly and quietly, and sitting and staying on command. This is the first step toward becoming a therapy dog and serving with your Bulldog in the community. Learn more at ww.akc.org/events/cgc.

• **AKC Therapy Dog Program:** This new AKC program rewards active, working therapy dogs with an official title, AKC ThD. To achieve the title, dogs and their handlers must be certified with recognized therapy dog associations, and regularly work to improve the lives of those in need and bring joy to all those they visit. For more information, visit www .akc.org/akctherapydog.

• **Pet Partners:** Professionally trained service animals are matched with people in need through this organization, depending on the emotional and physical needs of the person and the abilities of the dog. Get more information at www.petpartners.org.

• **Therapy Dogs, Inc.:** This organization provides dog-and-handler teams with registration, support, and insurance while they're involved with and participating in animal-assisted volunteer activities. To learn more, visit the website www.therapydogs.com.

• **Therapy Dogs International:** Qualified volunteers use this nonprofit group to help find facilities and institutions in need of certified therapy dogs. If you and your Bulldog are a certified therapy team, refer to this organization to help find appropriate assignments. Go to www.tdi-dog.org to find out more.

PROTECT YOUR BULLDOG

No matter what activities you get involved in with your Bulldog, don't forget that he has limitations due to the physical characteristics of his breed. Be mindful of his sensitivity to temperature and his need for multiple rests and breaks. Enjoy the activities for the fun of participation, but don't push your Bulldog to be a champion of obedience or agility. He is already a champion of the heart; love and protect your Bulldog for who he is, and he will love and protect you right back.

At a Glance ...

Keep your Bulldog active with regular walks and play sessions, which will keep him physically and mentally fit. The type of exercise that your Bulldog will enjoy most is anything that the two of you can do together!

You and your Bulldog can participate in many different types of organized activities, including conformation, obedience and agility competition, and more. Check out the websites of the American Kennel Club (www.akc.org) and the Bulldog Club of America (www.thebca.org) for more information on how to get involved in organized dog sports.

Therapy work is a great option for all Bulldogs that love meeting new people. Bring a smile to those in need by certifying your Bulldog as a therapy dog.

No matter what sport you participate in, be sure that your Bulldog is physically able to safely participate. Don't overwhelm your Bulldog with too much exercise or excitement; protect your Bulldog by talking with your veterinarian before participating in any physically demanding activities.

Resources

BOOKS

The American Kennel Club's Meet the Breeds: Dog Breeds from A to Z
(Irvine, California: BowTie Press, 2011) The ideal puppy buyer's guide, the 2012 edition of this book has all you need to know about each breed currently recognized by the AKC.

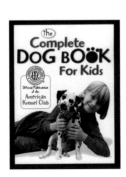

The Complete Dog Book, 20th edition (New York: Ballantine Books, 2006) This official publication of the AKC, first published in 1929, includes the complete histories and breed standards of 153 recognized breeds, as well as information on general care and the dog sport.

The Complete Dog Book for Kids (New York: Howell Book House, 1996) Specifically geared toward young people, this official publication of the AKC presents 149 breeds and varieties, as well as introductory owners' information.

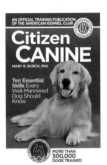

Citizen Canine: Ten Essential Skills Every Well-Mannered Dog Should Know by Mary R. Burch, PhD (Freehold, New Jersey: Kennel Club Books, 2010) This official AKC publication is the definitive guide to the AKC's Canine Good Citizen® program, recognized as the gold standard of behavior for dogs, with more than half a million dogs trained.

DOGS: The First 125 Years of the American Kennel Club (Freehold, New Jersey: Kennel Club Books, 2009) This official AKC publication presents an authoritative, complete history of the AKC, including detailed information not found in any other volume.

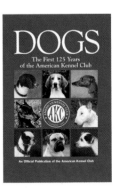

Dog Heroes of September 11: A Tribute to America's Search and Rescue Dogs, 10th anniversary edition, by Nona Kilgore Bauer (Freehold, New Jersey: Kennel Club Books, 2011) A publication to salute the canines that served in the recovery missions following the September 11th attacks, this book serves as a lasting tribute to these noble American heroes.

The Original Dog Bible: The Definitive Source for All Things Dog, 2nd edition, by Kristin Mehus-Roe (Irvine, California: BowTie Press, 2009) This 831-page magnum opus includes more than 250 breed profiles, hundreds of color photographs, and a wealth of information on every dog topic imaginable—thousands of practical tips on grooming, training, care, and much more.

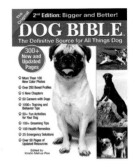

PERIODICALS

American Kennel Club Gazette

Every month since 1889, serious dog fanciers have looked to the *AKC Gazette* for authoritative advice on training, showing, breeding, and canine health. Each issue includes the breed columns section, written by experts from the respective breed clubs. Only available electronically.

AKC Family Dog

This is a bi-monthly magazine for the dog lover whose special dog is "just a pet." Helpful tips, how-tos, and features are written in an entertaining and reader-friendly format. It's a lifestyle magazine for today's busy families who want to enjoy a rewarding, mutually happy relationship with their canine companions.

Dog Fancy

The world's most widely read dog magazine, *Dog Fancy* celebrates dogs and the people who love them. Each monthly issue includes info on cutting-edge medical developments, health and fitness (with a focus on prevention, treatment, and natural therapy), behavior and training, travel and activities, breed profiles and dog news, and issues and trends for purebred and mixed-breed dog owners. The magazine informs, inspires, and entertains while promoting responsible dog ownership. Throughout its more than forty-year history, *Dog Fancy* has garnered numerous honors, including being named the Best All-Breed Magazine by the Dog Writers Association of America.

Dog World

With more than ninety-five years of tradition as the top magazine for active people with active dogs, *Dog World* provides authoritative, valuable, and entertaining content to the community of

serious dog enthusiasts and participants, including breeders; conformation exhibitors; obedience, agility, herding, and field trial competitors; veterinarians; groomers; and trainers. This monthly magazine is the resource to turn to for up-to-date information about canine health, advanced training, holistic and homeopathic methods, breeding, and conformation and performance sports.

Dogs in Review

For more than fifteen years, *Dogs in Review* has showcased the finest dogs in the U.S. and from around the world. The emphasis has always been on strong editorial content, with input from distinguished breeders, judges, and handlers worldwide. This global perspective distinguishes this monthly publication from its competitors—no other North American dog-show magazine gathers together so many international experts to enlighten and entertain its readership.

Dogs USA

Dogs USA is an annual lifestyle magazine published by the editors of *Dog Fancy* that covers all aspects of the dog world: culture, art, history, travel, sports, and science. It also profiles breeds to help prospective owners choose the best dogs for their future needs, such as a potential show champion, super service dog, great pet, or competitive star.

Natural Dog

Natural Dog is the magazine dedicated to giving a dog a natural lifestyle. From nutritional choices to grooming to dog-supply options, this publication helps readers make the transition from traditional

to natural methods. The magazine also explores the array of complementary treatments available for today's dogs: acupuncture, massage, homeopathy, aromatherapy, and much more. *Natural Dog* appears as an annual publication and also as the flip side of *Dog Fancy* magazine four times a year (in February, May, August, and November).

Puppies USA

Also from the editors of *Dog Fancy,* this annual magazine offers essential information for all new puppy owners. *Puppies USA* is lively and informative, including advice on general care, nutrition, grooming, and training techniques for all puppies, whether purebred or mixed breed, adopted, rescued, or purchased. In addition, it offers family fun through quizzes, contests, and much more. An extensive breeder directory is included.

WEBSITES

www.akc.org

The American Kennel Club's (AKC's) website is an excellent starting point for researching dog breeds and learning about puppy care. The site lists hundreds of breeders, along with basic information about breed selection and basic care. The site also has links to the national breed club of every AKC-recognized breed; breed-club sites offer plenty of detailed breed information, as well as lists of member breeders. In addition, you can find the AKC National Breed Club Rescue List at www.akc.org/breeds/rescue.cfm. If looking for purebred puppies, go to www.puppybuyerinfo.com for AKC classifieds and parent club referrals.

www.dogchannel.com

Dog Channel is "the website for dog lovers," where hundreds of thousands of visitors each month find extensive information on breeds, training, health and nutrition, puppies, care, activities, and more. Interactive features include forums, Dog College, games, puzzles, and Club Dog, an exclusive free club where dog lovers can create blogs for their pets and earn points to buy products. DogChannel is the definitive one-stop site for all things dog.

www.meetthebreeds.com

The official website of the AKC Meet the Breeds® event, hosted by the American Kennel Club in the Jacob Javits Center in New York City in the fall. The first Meet the Breeds event took place in 2009. The website includes information on every recognized breed of dog and cat, alphabetically listed, as well as the breeders, demonstration facilitators, sponsors, and vendors participating in the annual event.

AKC AFFILIATES

The **AKC Museum of the Dog**, established in 1981, is located in St. Louis, Missouri, and houses the world's finest collection of art devoted to the dog. Visit www.museumofthedog.org.

The **AKC Humane Fund** promotes the joy and value of responsible and productive pet ownership through education, outreach, and grant-making. Monies raised may fund grants to organizations that teach responsible pet ownership; provide for the health and well-being of all dogs; and preserve and celebrate the human-animal bond and the evolutionary relationship between dogs and humankind. Go to www.akchumanefund.org.

The **American Kennel Club Companion Animal Recovery (CAR) Corporation** is dedicated to reuniting lost microchipped and tattooed pets with their owners. AKC CAR maintains a permanent-identification database and provides lifetime recovery services 24 hours a day, 365 days a year, for all animal species. Millions of pets are enrolled in the program, which was established in 1995. Visit www.akccar.org.

The **American Kennel Club Canine Health Foundation (AKC CHF), Inc.** is the largest foundation in the world to fund canine-only health studies for purebred and mixed-breed dogs. More than $22 million has been allocated in research funds to more than 500 health studies conducted to help dogs live longer, healthier lives. Go to www.akcchf.org.

AKC PROGRAMS

The **Canine Good Citizen Program (CGC)** was established in 1989 and is designed to recognize dogs that have good manners at home and in the community. This rapidly growing, nationally recognized program stresses responsible dog ownership for owners and basic training and good manners for dogs. All dog that pass the ten-step Canine Good Citizen test receive a certificate from the American Kennel Club. Go to www.akc.org/events/cgc.

The **AKC S.T.A.R. Puppy Program** is designed to get dog owners and their puppies off to a good start and is aimed at loving dog owners who have taken the time to attend basic obedience classes with their puppies. After completing a six-week training course, the puppy must pass the AKC S.T.A.R. Puppy test, which evaluates Socialization, Training, Activity, and Responsibility. Go to www.akc.org/starpuppy.

The **AKC Therapy Dog** program recognizes all American Kennel Club dogs and their owners who have given their time and helped people by volunteering as a therapy dog-and-owner team. The AKC Therapy Dog program is an official American Kennel Club title awarded to dogs who have worked to improve the lives of the people they have visited. The AKC Therapy Dog title (AKC ThD) can be earned by dogs who have been certified by recognized therapy dog organizations. Visit www.akc.org/akctherapydog.

Index

AMERICAN KENNEL CLUB®

Advocating for the purebred dog as a family companion, advancing canine health and well-being, working to protect the rights of all dog owners and promoting responsible dog ownership, the **American Kennel Club:**

Sponsors more than **22,000 sanctioned events** annually including conformation, agility, obedience, rally, tracking, lure coursing, earthdog, herding, field trial, hunt test, and coonhound events

Features a **10-step Canine Good Citizen® program** that rewards dogs who have good manners at home and in the community

Has reunited more than **400,000** lost pets with their owners through the AKC Companion Animal Recovery - visit **www.akccar.org**

Created and supports the AKC Canine Health Foundation, which funds research projects using the more than **$22 million** the AKC has donated since 1995 - visit **www.akcchf.org**

Joins **animal lovers** through education, outreach and grant-making via the AKC Humane Fund - visit **www.akchumanefund.org**

We're more than champion dogs. We're the dog's champion.

www.akc.org